MW01234698

INSPIRE GOOD

Nonprofit Marketing for a Better World

BILL WEGER

A portion of the royalties received from sales of this book
will be donated to charities.

INSPIRE GOOD ® is a registered trademark of
Image One PR Consulting, LLC

Order this book online at www.trafford.com
or email orders@trafford.com

Most Trafford titles are also available at major online book retailers.

Printed in the United States of America.

ISBN: 978-1-4269-8908-7 (sc)
ISBN: 978-1-4269-8910-0 (hc)
ISBN: 978-1-4269-8909-4 (e)

Library of Congress Control Number: 2011914848

Trafford rev. 12/05/2011

 www.trafford.com

North America & international
toll-free: 1 888 232 4444 (USA & Canada)
phone: 250 383 6864 ♦ fax: 812 355 4082

Contents

Part IV: Promoting Good Causes

Part V: New and Social Media

Preface: A Book of Inspiration

In the heart of every community, you'll find nonprofits hard at work. Helping neighbors. Feeding the hungry. Caring for the sick. Making lives better. Nonprofits fill critical gaps, shape policy, mobilize stakeholders, and contribute to the economy.

These are the hallmarks of America's nonprofits. And behind every nonprofit are remarkable stories that need telling. This book is for nonprofit marketing professionals who want to tell their organization's stories so people listen and take action. It's meant to be a handy resource filled with strategies and practical tips for improving nonprofit marketing and communications. It's intended to start conservations, facilitate open communications, and drive measurable outcomes for nonprofit organizations. Foremost, the purpose of this publication is to *inspire good*.

More than 25 years ago, when I began my communications career, I went to work for three years at the American Red Cross National Headquarters in Washington, D.C. It was a meaningful experience that shaped my opinion that the nonprofit marketer's primary job is to *inspire good* – whether it's raising funds, increasing awareness, influencing behavior, or recruiting volunteers. It all boils down to getting people to take positive action that makes a difference.

 In 2002, I founded Image One PR with a focus on serving nonprofits, associations, and government. Consistent with our work, we decided our tagline would be inspire good® – also the title of this book. Over the years, I

conducted presentations before nonprofit audiences and wrote a series of articles for our newsletter entitled, *Brand Bytes*. The topics covered a range of marketing and public relations areas, including naming, branding, logo development, website development, media relations, micromarketing, and much more.

So I always had an outline for a book in my head. I finally put it all together in the form of this publication, adding fresh information and many new thoughts and ideas. I have been fortunate to work for and with diverse nonprofits small and large, including the American Red Cross, the Epilepsy Foundation, Lutheran Services in America, Mothers Against Drunk Driving, and the W.K. Kellogg Foundation.

Much of what I learned over two decades as a journalist, nonprofit marketer, association professional, government contractor, and volunteer has gone into writing this book. I have tried to share information that will be valuable to nonprofit marketers with limited staff, budget, and resources.

I hope this simple book helps you to *inspire good*. Best wishes in your efforts to strengthen nonprofits and achieve their critical missions.

About the Author

Bill Weger is the Founder and Senior Partner of Image One PR, a social marketing and strategic communications firm that specializes in nonprofits, associations, healthcare, education, and government.

Based in Rockville, Maryland, Image One PR has received 30 national and international awards for communications excellence, including Ava, APEX, Aster, Aurora, Communicator, Hermes Creative, MarCom, and Telly Awards.

For more than 20 years, Bill has worked for or with some of the nation's most respected nonprofit organizations and government agencies, including the American Red Cross, The Epilepsy Foundation, Lutheran Services in America, W.K. Kellogg Foundation, the U.S. Department of Health and Human Services, and the U.S. Department of Housing and Urban Development.

He has created and successfully executed nationally recognized branding, social marketing, and public awareness campaigns. Bill speaks and conducts workshops on nonprofit marketing at national conferences.

He earned a Bachelor of Science degree in Journalism from the University of Maryland, College Park and a Master of Arts degree in Public Communications from The American University in Washington, D.C. He has been a member of the Public Relations Society of America since 1989. He is also a member of the American Public Health Association.

Bill enjoys reading, running, poetry, and spending time with his wife and family. You can reach him through the Image One PR website at www.imageonepr.com.

How to Use This Book

This book was written specifically for nonprofit marketers who need a handy resource they can turn to for proven strategies, quick reads, and guidance. Whether you are an Executive Director, Communications Manager, Marketing Assistant, Development Director, or Volunteer, this book is meant for you.

Put it on your desk. Keep it on your bookshelf. Share it with your colleagues. It's for you to use when and where it has the most value. Read it once. Make mental notes. And refer to it often when seeking solutions for your next nonprofit marketing challenge.

This book is organized into five parts. Together, they present a multi-faceted and open approach to achieving effective nonprofit marketing and communications.

Part I: The New Nonprofit Marketing Environment provides fresh insights on the nonprofit marketing landscape today and how it's rapidly changing. The section outlines seven strategies for success and the role nonprofit marketers play as social butterflies. The influence and benefits of social marketing are also discussed, along with cause marketing and micromarketing. Part I also offers strategies for creating a marketing plan true to your mission. The section includes a Network for Good case study on optimizing online giving.

Part II: Building Brand Connections highlights ways to strengthen your nonprofit's position and visibility. Important topics covered in this section include the six pillars of branding (research, visualize, verbalize, promote, protect, and refine), repositioning, naming, taglines, logos, the psychology of colors, and great design for good causes. Part II also presents a case study in effective nonprofit branding.

Part III: Nonprofit Communications: Let's Talk encourages nonprofits to build successful relationships through open communications and conversations. This section highlights the importance of articulating your vision and mission, shaping messages that stick, the language of nonprofits, multicultural communications, website content development, and why telling great stories is vital to connecting with stakeholders.

Part IV: Promoting Good Causes gives you strategies and tips for increasing stakeholder awareness and earning positive marketing results. You will learn about nonprofit public relations in a Web 2.0 world, developing a media plan with traction, the power of public service announcements, cultivating media relationships, becoming word on the street, creating special events, the rise of citizen journalism, and why traditional media, and aging news releases still matter. This section also highlights an award-winning national media campaign that helped Lutheran Services in America boost its national profile and raise funds through its online auction, Trading Graces.

Part V: New and Social Media recognizes the value of facilitating conversations in the new era of public engagement. This section focuses on ways to help your nonprofit leverage social media as a tool for listening, sharing, and facilitating conversations. Topics discussed here include creating a social media strategy, connecting with the Facebook and Twitter communities, blogging to say something, broadcasting on YouTube, Flickr for nonprofits, and mobile marketing.

PART I

The New Nonprofit Marketing Environment

Chapter 1

The Evolution of Nonprofit Marketing

Good actions give strength to ourselves and inspire good actions in others.
– Plato

While answering pledge phones for the Jerry Lewis MDA Labor Day Telethon one year, a woman asked me "Where would we be without volunteers and nonprofits like the MDA?"

It reminded me of the holiday film classic "It's a Wonderful Life" when Clarence the Angel tells George Bailey (Jimmy Stewart) that he has been given a great gift – a chance to see what the world would be like without him.

"One man's life touches so many others, when he's not here it leaves an awfully big hole," Clarence says profoundly. To demonstrate the point, the story recounts how, as a child, George Bailey saved his brother from falling through the ice and drowning. Later in life, his brother, Harry, went on to become a Navy fighter pilot and was awarded the Medal of Honor for shooting down enemy aircraft, including one that would have crashed into a U.S. transport ship full of troops.

What if there were no charitable organizations? Imagine the enormous hardships, despair, and lost dreams. When "It's a Wonderful Life" premiered in 1946, fewer than 100,000 nonprofit organizations existed in the United States.

The nonprofit sector today is bigger, more complex, and organized than ever before. Simultaneously, the role of nonprofit marketers has never been more important. Today, more than 1.4 million nonprofits, foundations, and religious congregations fill gaps, save lives, and do the selfless work and giving that makes our lives, communities, and world better.

According to the Corporation for National and Community Service, 62.8 million Americans volunteered to help their communities in 2010, providing powerful economic and social benefits to communities across the nation. These volunteers contributed 8.1 billion hours of service with an estimated equivalent dollar value of $169 billion. More than 10 percent of the American workforce is employed by nonprofits, which contribute nearly $322 billion in wages, according to a study by the Johns Hopkins University Center for Civil Society Studies. These facts are a remarkable testament to the spirit of serving others for the greater good and their importance to the economy.

The Era of Public Engagement

The nonprofit landscape has undergone dramatic change over the past 100 years and new technologies and sophisticated communication forms have fueled its growth and success. Nonprofit marketing and public relations, along with radio, television, cable, and the Internet, have all played important roles in the sector's enormous expansion. And now, social media is the new game changer.

Today, the social media revolution is creating exciting new opportunities for nonprofits to engage the public in online conversation and content sharing. From Twitter, Facebook, and Flickr to Wikipedia and the blogosphere, the remarkable and rapid proliferation of Web 2.0 and new media has reached a "tipping point."

In 2000, several years before new and social media became a worldwide phenomenon, Malcolm Gladwell wrote a best-selling book, *"The Tipping Point: How Little Things Can Make a Big Difference."* Tipping points, according to Gladwell, are the levels at which the momentum for change is unstoppable. Clearly, the acceptance and affinity for social media has reached critical mass.

In many ways, the butterfly principal reflects the ripple effect of the social media revolution. Based in chaos theory, the butterfly principle supports the idea that small differences can collectively create a big difference over time. For example, the flapping of a butterfly's wings produces a tiny change in the state of the atmosphere that can change weather patterns. So a huge migration of butterflies to Mexico can potentially cause a tornado in Texas.

Similarly, social media participation started slowly, but over several years a metamorphosis occurred. Perceptions changed. The caterpillar became a butterfly and a popular communication form with worldwide influence.

Becoming Social Butterflies

In a sense, nonprofit marketers serve as social butterflies. Think of the flight of the butterfly. It goes from flower to flower, garden to garden, and meadow to meadow gathering nectar. Each visit, no matter how short, is purposeful and promotes the cycle of nature.

Today's nonprofit marketers play the role of social butterflies determined to glean something from each conversation. Effective nonprofit marketers listen, respond, and work hard to start conversations and connect with many stakeholders across diverse cultures and environments. The goal is learning something new from each encounter.

Social media, conversation by conversation, is changing the way we communicate. It's opening new doors to collaboration, relationship building, and engagement. For some nonprofits and businesses, the challenge is realizing that they can no longer control the message. The good news is that nonprofits get it and they are increasingly embracing social media.

Nonprofits Saying "Yes" to Social Media

According to an April 2011 survey conducted by NTEN, Common Knowledge, and Blackbaud, 89 percent of nonprofits now have a Facebook presence and 57 percent are on Twitter.

The new and social media statistics are simply mind-boggling.

- 77% of U.S. population online.
- 800 million + worldwide on Facebook.
- 13% of U.S population using Twitter.
- 48 hours of video uploaded to YouTube every minute.
- 3.8 million articles on English Wikipedia.
- 177 million public blogs.
- 5 billion photos on Flickr.

Advantages to Social Media

So why have nonprofit organizations embraced social media? Primarily, they're using social media to listen better, increase awareness, engage stakeholders, inspire action, strengthen their brand, increase online donations, and attract volunteers. Associations are turning to social media to increase member retention, attract new members, influence policy, increase non-dues revenues, offer interactive events, and promote thought leadership. Traditional media, which are still influential, use social media to strengthen ties with readers, increase online advertising, and provide a venue for interactive, two-way communication.

Social media is a powerful force for change. It's all about conversations and full public engagement. It represents a new era in nonprofit marketing that blends traditional ways of marketing and communicating with unprecedented opportunities to interact and share with stakeholders.

Social media expands our ability to hold conversations, socialize, discover, disseminate information, share opinions, thoughts, and content using easily accessible and scalable publishing technologies. It gives a voice to participants and provides a dynamic channel to facilitate open, interactive communications.

The Impact on Traditional Media

Meanwhile, the social media revolution has splintered audiences and negatively impacted other traditional forms of media, such as newspapers and television. Industries that are generally considered part of the traditional media are broadcast and cable television, radio, film, newspapers, books, magazines, and outdoor advertising. Many of those industries are now less profitable than they used to be due in part to the growth of new media.

For example, the number of nightly news viewers has shrunk from approximately 53 million in 1981 when Walter Cronkite retired as the CBS Evening News anchor to less than 23 million today. Newspapers are thinner, lighter, and losing subscribers at a record pace. Total U.S. newspaper circulation has declined for more than two decades. Just two in five or roughly 43 percent of U.S. adults are regular readers of newspapers.

Sadly enough, many people could simply live without newspapers. A 2009 Pew Research Center for the People & Press survey noted that fewer than half of Americans (43%) say that losing their local newspaper would hurt civic life in their community "a lot."

According to a 2010 Pew Internet & American Life Report, slightly more than half of American adults (56%) say they follow the news "all or most of the time." The report noted that 92% of all Americans follow the news daily on multiple platforms. On a typical day, 78% of Americans get news from a local TV station; 73% get news from a national television network; 61% from online news sources; 54% listen to a radio news program; 50% read news in the print version of a local newspaper and 17% read news in a print version national newspaper, such as the *Wall Street Journal* or *USA Today*.

So how we get our news varies widely. It's important for nonprofit marketers to stay up with the latest news consumption habits to better understand audiences and how to best reach them. Despite the social media buzz, traditional media still have a leading role in message delivery, increasing awareness, changing behavior, and framing issues. Many leading decision-makers and influencers still read newspapers, watch the news, and listen to the radio.

Breaking Through the Noise

Clearly, social media is having an effect on our culture and daily habits; just as the Internet, the 24-hour news cycle, the *USA Today*, and television did when they entered the American scene.

But what does it all mean? The emerging social media environment and an overload of daily messages have caused a traffic jam in our minds. In effect, it's now harder than ever to get the word out about an issue. It's even tougher for messages to stick. The good news is that people still listen and act when the message is relevant and timely. It's all about striking a responsive chord on a personal or emotional level. The best way to break through all the noise is often integrating traditional media tactics with select social media strategies. It's the new public relations model in the era of public engagement.

Government Leveraging Social Media

Like nonprofits, political candidates and the federal government, too, are increasingly using social media. President Barack Obama understands social media and the Internet like Presidents John F. Kennedy and Ronald Reagan got the power of television. President Obama ushered in a new digital era in presidential fundraising, raising a record half billion dollars online during his campaign. More than two million people created online profiles on barackobama.com.

In 2010, many federal websites were redesigned with a fresh look and new social media tools. For instance, the Government Accountability Office uses Twitter and YouTube to inform the public about its reports and mission. The Library of Congress has collaborated with Flickr to increase awareness of Library of Congress materials and most agencies now have their own Facebook pages.

Promoting Public Health

One of the greatest potential benefits of social media, for nonprofits and government alike, is the ability to increase awareness of public health issues. Through new and traditional media, vital health information can travel far and fast.

Increasingly, Americans are going online to get their healthcare information. In September 2010, a Pew Research Center survey showed that 80 percent of American adults looked online for health information. More than 500,000 Americans searched online for Swine Flu at the height of the outbreak in April 2009, according to comSCORE.

Social networking sites are also visited for health information, but not nearly as often as more traditional online and offline sources. One obstacle is ensuring that the public is getting accurate information from a reliable source.

While many Americans still prefer information directly from health professionals, some are reading blogs, listening to podcasts, and posting comments. The Pew Internet/California Healthcare Foundation survey found that technology is not an end, but a means to further explore and learn about health issues.

An Everyday Health Widget

The U.S. Department of Health and Human Services (HHS) sees new media, which can be monitored and analyzed for effectiveness, as an opportunity to increase public health awareness and alert consumers about potential health threats. In 2010, for example, The Centers for Disease Control and Prevention (CDC) and the U.S. Food and Drug Administration (FDA) used social media to warn consumers about a salmonella outbreak caused by contaminated eggs.

Federal health agencies are using a variety of social and new media tools, including blogs, podcasts, health e-cards, webinars, and widgets. A CDC widget is an e-health tool that allows you to embed content in personalized home pages, blogs, and other sites. This innovative application provides you updated content automatically, including a Weekly Influenza Surveillance Report. In addition, the CDC maintains social network profiles on Facebook and Twitter. The public can also subscribe to HHS Really Simple Syndication (RSS) feeds to get ongoing health news.

Whether it's the CDC, the MDA, or the LIVESTRONG Foundation sharing new research findings and medical information, social media has enormous potential to impact and improve public health.

The Future in Focus

The evolution of the Internet has created unprecedented opportunities to engage audiences in interactive, two-way communication. Nonprofits, associations, and government agencies are increasingly adding social media strategies to their marketing and public awareness campaigns.

And while new media is all the rage, traditional media, such as television, newspapers, magazines, and radio, still play a powerful role in framing issues, raising awareness, and inspiring action. Like it or not social media are here to stay and traditional media will adjust and survive. The two media forms will co-exist and those organizations and individuals that can take advantage of both traditional and new media will be the most connected.

Leveraging Social Media: American Red Cross Success

Imagine earthquake disaster victims, like those in Haiti, trapped under debris desperately texting for help on Facebook and Twitter. Is anyone listening and can they respond? The use of social media during and after the massive earthquake sent a clear signal that new technology has prompted a major shift in disaster response. In August 2010, the American Red Cross hosted an Emergency Social Data Summit to discuss better ways to handle information that flows through the web during a disaster. A Red Cross survey showed that many web users would turn to social media to seek help for themselves or others during an emergency, and they expect first responders to be listening.

The online survey asked 1,058 adults about their use of social media sites in emergency situations. It found that if they needed help and could not reach 9-1-1, one in five would try to contact responders through digital means, such as email, websites, or social media. The survey noted that 44 percent would ask other people in their social network to contact authorities, 35 percent would post a request for help directly on a response agency's Facebook page and 28 percent would send direct Twitter messages to responders.

And survey respondents expected quick response to an online appeal for help – 69 percent of respondents expect emergency responders to be monitoring social media sites and 74 percent expected help to come less than an hour after their tweet or Facebook post. The survey found that among web users, social media sites are the fourth most popular source for emergency information, just behind television news, radio, and online news sites.

Becoming Better Listeners

Every day, several hundred people talk online about how their lives interact with the Red Cross, according to Wendy Harman, Red Cross Director of Social Strategy. In 2006, the Red Cross became an early adopter of social media in the aftermath of Hurricane Katrina. The Red Cross wanted to listen better, measure outreach efforts, and respond to negative comments. Social media presented the perfect tool for joining the conversations and engaging supporters, Harman said.

Today, Red Cross leverages the power of the social web to raise awareness, connect with donors, raise disaster relief funds, cultivate the next generation of supporters, and understand how the organization can better support the communities it serves. "Red Cross uses social media as a tool to empower stakeholders and fulfill our mission," Harman said. "Social media helps us to listen and pay attention to the people who support us. We ask ourselves daily how do we engage people and invite them to participate and take action?"

More than 390,000 people like the Red Cross Facebook page and more than 575,000 people are Red Cross Twitter followers. Hundreds of Red Cross videos are posted on the nonprofit organization's YouTube site. More than 5,000 photos are posted to the Red Cross Flickr site, including many historic photos highlighting the early years of the nearly 130-year-old organization. The Red Cross blogs everyday, covering diverse topics, including emergency preparedness, health, safety, and volunteerism.

At the heart of social media success is listening and responding to people who care about your organization and its mission, said Harman, who believes social media is here to stay and new technologies will expand conversations and create unprecedented opportunities to engage stakeholders in ways never before possible.

Chapter 2

Modern Marketing Many Ways

Action is the foundational key to all success.
– Pablo Picasso

Every year, marketing evolves. It changes with marketplace needs, advancing technologies, social trends, economic conditions, and fresh new approaches to connecting with audiences. Long gone are the days when many nonprofit organizations simply can disseminate information, such as newsletters and brochures, to stakeholders with little interaction and feedback.

Today, nonprofit marketing is dynamic and multi-faceted. Each new challenge requires taking a unique and tailored approach to achieve the best results. It's applying modern marketing many ways.

Nonprofits have always been cost-conscious and using the right marketing mix can stretch your budget dollars. This becomes even more of a reality during tough economic periods. During financial downturns, many nonprofits feel the financial pinch of steep budget cuts at the state and county levels, a drop in individual donations, fewer foundation grants, and limited corporate contributions. Competition for funding and resources becomes stiff.

Turbulent economic environments force many nonprofits to make hard decisions – whether it's scaling back programs, reducing staff, or delaying initiatives. Faced with small and sometimes shrinking budgets, marketing and communications departments are often challenged to "do more with less."

Whether the economy is up or down, it doesn't have to stop your organization from achieving high-impact goals. Now may be the best time to focus on strategic communications and position your nonprofit for the future. At the very least, your organization will be poised to take advantage of the next big opportunity.

Here are some hard questions to ponder. Is your nonprofit truly connecting with donors in all the ways it can? Are you cultivating relationships with those key entities that provide funding streams? Is your nonprofit forgotten, or are you fighting to stay in the public eye?

Get creative and employ new strategies and tactics that will help your nonprofit organization overcome barriers to success. Several timely and effective strategies to weigh include:

- Forging new corporate partnerships.
- Focusing on measurement.
- Storytelling to share success.
- Refining the brand.
- Re-evaluating messaging.
- Revisiting the website.
- Engaging in social media to increase awareness, engage audiences, inspire action, increase online donations, and attract volunteers.

Nonprofits with vision are always looking ahead. They ensure that strategic marketing and communications are at the heart of any effort to build long-term sustainability and strength. Successful nonprofits use the tactics and tools of modern marketing to their full advantage. Today, the options are plentiful, thanks to new media, improved technologies, and a rapidly changing communications environment.

Marketing today grows increasingly complex and conversational. It's much more than sending out messages to a mass market, hoping something sticks. Modern marketing is about participation, relationships, and dialogue. Modern marketing takes many forms. Just to name a few: micromarketing, direct marketing, social marketing, cause marketing, integrated marketing, and even neuromarketing, which studies cognitive and affective response to marketing stimuli.

Defining Marketing and Public Relations

So how do we define marketing and public relations (PR) and what does it mean for nonprofit organizations? According to the American Marketing Association, marketing is the activity, set of institutions, and processes for creating, communicating, delivering, and exchanging offerings that have value for customers, clients, partners, and society at large.

In the nonprofit world, marketing must be relevant and offer some sort of value to stakeholders – whether it's emotional or tangible. Modern marketing goes beyond promoting goods and services. Effective marketing attracts attention, inspires action, builds trust, reinforces your brand, and strengthens long-term sustainability.

It advances your mission and aligns your organizational goals with the needs of your stakeholders who want to feel good about their investment or commitment. The exchange focuses on giving and getting something back in return. A volunteer donates his or her time and feels good knowing they made a difference. Simultaneously, your organization furthers its mission. It becomes a win-win for everyone.

As a mature and influential marketing discipline, PR should never be underestimated. PR must play a central role in advancing your nonprofit's mission. In the new social media era, PR has changed dramatically and will continue to evolve. Today, PR has been reinvented, moving more to an open communications model with greater stakeholder participation. Shared content is in. Message control is out.

Modern PR holds value best when it can foster positive relationships, increase awareness, extend your brand, drive measurable outcomes, and empower participants – whether they are donors, partners, volunteers, or recipients of services.

PR has been portrayed and defined in many ways since its formal beginnings in the early 1900s. In 1982, the Public Relations Society of America (PRSA) adopted a definition of public relations that remains widely accepted and used today. "Public relations helps an organization and its publics adapt mutually to each other."

According to PRSA, "organization" includes businesses, trade unions, government agencies, voluntary associations, foundations, hospitals, schools, and colleges. Publics recognizes the need to understand the attitudes and values of many different stakeholders, including employees, members, donors, volunteers, and local communities. It's important that your nonprofit builds relationships with these key stakeholders. On a personal note, this author has been a PRSA member for more than 20 years, and I can attest to its excellence, particularly in its support of the non-profit sector.

More Two-Way Communication

Modern PR born of the social media age embraces relationship building and understanding stakeholder needs and values much more than in previous eras. While attending the College of Journalism at the University of Maryland in the 1980s, I studied the history of the four models of public relations, as researched by James E. Grunig (University of Maryland) and Todd Hunt (University of Rutgers) and written about in their book, *"Managing Public Relations."*

The four models are:

(1) press agent/publicity model (1850 to 1900)
(2) public information model (1900-1920s)
(3) two-way asymmetric model (developed in 1920s)
(4) asymmetric model (begun 1960s and 1970s)

The first three models focus primarily on one-way communication (sending out information, such as news releases and press kits, and using persuasion and manipulation to influence audiences without using research to identify their attitudes and opinions about the organization.) Some of the nation's largest and most influential nonprofits, including the American Red Cross and YMCA, really came of age during the one-way communication period.

In contrast, the two-way symmetrical model uses communication to negotiate with publics, resolve conflict, promote understanding, and a mutually beneficial relationship. It's important to know how public relations has evolved over the past century and just how rapidly it's being reinvented before our eyes – presenting many more two-way opportunities to interact with stakeholders. Today, social media gives nonprofits more tools and channels to facilitate open communication, active engagement, and immediate feedback from stakeholders.

Paving the Way to Modern PR

Edward Bernays and Ivy Lee are recognized as early pioneers in public relations who paved way for many of today's current practices. Their influential work in the 1900s played an important role in the development of public relations as a profession. Bernays was the profession's first theorist and is widely-regarded as the father of public relations. He was a nephew of psychoanalyst Sigmund Freud.

Bernays, who lived to the ripe old age of 103, viewed public relations as a social science influenced by psychology, sociology, and other disciplines. He attempted to manipulate public opinion through the subconscious. He believed public relations, as a social science, could be used to scientifically manage and manipulate public thinking and behavior of an irrational public. He compared the publics to a herd waiting to be led.

Coincidently, at the University of Maryland, my degree in journalism (public relations sequence) is a bachelor of science, as opposed to arts. Our course of study required taking social science courses in history, sociology, and psychology. My graduate degree in public communications from American University is a master of arts. Personally, I view public relations as both social science and arts.

Bernays saw public relations as a management function – much as it still is viewed today. He felt public relations should measure public attitudes, define policies, and develop programs aimed at earning public understanding and acceptance. Even today, in both the independent and private-sectors, an effective public relations program strives to achieve these goals. Bernays' 1923 groundbreaking book, *"Crystalizing Public Opinion,"* helped to shape the role of public relations as a management function that serves to form public opinion and increase understanding. Whether your nonprofit communications team is comprised of one person or 15, it should be respected as a management function that advances your organization's mission.

More than 100 years ago, Ivy Lee developed the first press release. Today, press releases are still a valuable public relations tool, whether you like them or not. Some historians also credit Lee for inventing modern crisis communications.

On October 28, 1906, at least 50 people were killed in the wake of a tragic Pennsylvania Railroad accident. Lee convinced the railroad, one of his clients, to issue a public statement. *The New York Times* was so impressed with the new approach that it printed the release verbatim. In the weeks that followed, newspapers and public officials praised Pennsylvania Railroad for its honesty and openness.

Lee, a former New York reporter, believed communications was a "two-way-street" and that listening, responding, and building public trust were keys to achieving successful public relations. University of Maryland Professor Emeritus Ray E. Hiebert, who was the dean of the College of Journalism when I was an undergraduate, wrote a biography about Lee, entitled, *"Courtier to the Crowd: The Story of Ivy Lee* (Iowa State University Press, 1966).

For many decades, news releases remained unchanged, although today they are often criticized for their hype and not sticking to the facts. Of course, as social media has evolved, so has the news release. Later in this book, you will learn more about Social Media Releases (SMRs). Long live news releases!

The main point to remember about Bernays and Lee is that they were innovative thinkers and trailblazers who brought greater respect to the PR profession. Their body of work and practices paved the way for advancement in the field. Nonprofit communicators who blend both traditional marketing and PR with modern strategies, tactics, and tools can achieve effective results.

Communications Plans True to Your Mission

Does your nonprofit have a mission? It probably does. Then it should have a strategic communications plan, too. The best nonprofit communications plans begin with the organization's mission in mind. Why do we exist? What is our purpose and how will our communications, marketing, and outreach efforts advance our cause? And while a good plan begins with the mission, it always stays focused on the organization's audiences.

Motivated stakeholders drive missions, whether it's protecting the environment, promoting peace, or something else. Good ıunications plans inspire people to take action. They get people come members, donate money, give their time, and spread the word. To inspire action, you must understand your audiences and know what makes them tick. Uncovering the attitudes, beliefs, and values of your audiences through research and listening will help you to find effective ways to satisfy their needs and wants. Only then can your communications efforts convert passive audiences into active stakeholders and strong supporters who advance your mission.

Effective communications plans serve as a blueprint for your nonprofit and help create excitement, engage stakeholders, build dialogue, attract loyal fans, recruit volunteers, raise funds, sell products and services, and extend your organization's brand. But remember to stay true to your mission.

Your nonprofit can't be all things to all people. It can't save the world, but it does have a unique place in making it better. Determine what makes your nonprofit special and bundle it so people embrace your mission. Remain committed to excellence every step of the way and build in quality control measures that ensure success.

How far ahead your communications plan reaches may depend on what you want to accomplish and when and whether it aligns with your nonprofit's strategic vision and mission. In a rapidly changing environment, a two-year communications plan may meet your needs. Your communications plan can and should be refined as needed. Don't leave it on a shelf or store it in your computer to gather dust.

Creating Effective Communications Plans

So what goes into creating a comprehensive communications plan? Different organizations use different approaches, but including the following 11 essential elements will give you a solid platform to build and refine your nonprofit communications plan.

11 Essential Communications Plan Elements

Element	*Content*
Executive Summary	An overview of your plan and its purpose
Communications Environment	The internal and external communications situation
Market Differentiators	What separates your nonprofit from the competition
Strategy	The big picture approach
Goals and Objectives	What you want your plan to do
Target Audiences	Who you want to reach with your message
Messages	What you say to inspire action
Communications Channels	The mediums for reaching audiences
Tactics	Specific activities for strategy implementation
Budget	Funds and resources to carry out the plan
Evaluation	How you measure outcomes and success

Executive Summary

The Executive Summary is a snapshot of the communications plan. It touches briefly on the plan's components and vision for implementation and success. Good executive summaries are short and sweet. Two or three pages should suffice.

Communications Environment

In this section, identify the circumstances under which your nonprofit's internal and external communications operate. Whether responding to the media, attracting volunteers, mobilizing stakeholders, or generating donations, nonprofits need to understand their strategic communications performance and how it impacts organizational success.

Some marketing professionals call this a Situational Analysis and others prefer to conduct a Strengths, Weaknesses, Opportunities, and Threats (SWOT) Analysis or a Communications Audit, which is a review and assessment of your nonprofit's communications effectiveness and capacity.

Whether a single or combined method is selected, you'll need to unfold the essence of how your organization communicates. Is communication open and more inclusive than exclusive? Does it facilitate two-way communication and the exchange of ideas? What factors are facilitating or hindering communications?

Much can be learned by reviewing existing communications practices and listening to what stakeholders are saying about your communications efforts. A full communications analysis will help you to:

- Determine if the communication needs of your organization are being met.
- Evaluate the effectiveness of communication channels and methods.
- Appraise the effectiveness and consistency of messages.
- Identify visibility and credibility challenges.

To assess the current communications environment, you'll need to conduct research. This may involve online surveys, focus groups, telephone and face-to-face interviews, analysis, product and service reviews, and other qualitative and quantitative research methodologies that help you gather the information you need.

Market Differentiators

Here you define what makes your organization remarkable. How does your nonprofit stand out from the crowd? Why does your nonprofit zig while others zag? What brand personality or characteristics are unique to your organization? By answering these questions, you can write a powerful Positioning Statement that conveys your nonprofit's distinct advantage over the competition based on the perceptions of your target audience. A well-crafted statement will help you to find a niche market in the hyper-competitive nonprofit arena.

Differentiators include a long-history, tradition, leadership, management, quality, speed, cost, market innovation, highly effective, or the uniqueness of service offerings. Determining your differentiators requires knowing the competition, the perceptions of your audiences, and what you have to offer others.

Strategy

The strategy represents the brains behind your communications plan. It drives the approach and direction you will take in implementing your plan. It might be complex and multi-layered, such as:

- Enhancing communication between the national office and chapters.
- Facilitating communication among members.
- Connecting with partners.
- Building an online community or social network.
- Promoting the brand.

Or it may just be a single strategy, such as increasing community awareness. The strategy should be drawn from insights, research findings, observations, and conclusions. Of course, your available budget will affect the extent of your strategy and your ability to carry it out.

Goals and Objectives

Part of your communications strategy should include setting goals and objectives. The primary goal should serve to advance your mission. This goal often focuses on inspiring audiences to take action. Supporting communications goals help to achieve the overarching goal over time. Several examples of supporting goals include:

- Fostering an open, interactive communications environment.
- Building the confidence and trust of member organizations by keeping them informed.
- Marketing and promoting services that audiences want and need.
- Encouraging audiences to feel they are part of a greater cause.
- Increasing name recognition and raising brand awareness.
- Influencing public policy.
- Moving the needle of public opinion by mobilizing audiences.

Specific objectives drill down deeper and often attempt to achieve measurable outcomes designed to further the supportive goals and the primary goal over a particular time. Specific goals may include:

- To generate 50 million media impressions annually through consistent and proactive media outreach.
- To build a social network of 5,000 followers and fans in six months.
- To increase the number of monthly website visits by 20 percent.

When establishing your goals and objectives, be realistic based on where you are now, your available budget, and the readiness of your audiences to take action.

Target Audiences

Target audiences should be the focus of your communications and outreach strategies and tactics. Whether through the telephone, a blog, a hotline, in a soup kitchen, at the mall, in school, or on the job, you need to connect with audiences where they live, work, and play, especially in places where they are in contact with or thinking about your nonprofit.

It helps to have insights about your audiences. Who are they? What interests them? How do they interact with your nonprofit and what are their needs, preferences, behaviors, attitudes, and characteristics? Where do they get information, and what are their media consumption habits? The success of your communications plan depends largely on implementing a program of consistent, open communications with audiences, who in turn, become spokespersons and messengers who can promote the value and benefits of your nonprofit.

Messages should be delivered to target audiences through the most effective communications channels and at the best time to strike an emotional chord or response. Of course, target audiences vary depending on the communications environment. Think about both internal and external audiences. Examples of internal audiences include staff, volunteers, board members, and affiliates. External audiences may include service recipients, service seekers, donors, potential volunteers, partners and corporate sponsors, lawmakers, government and community leaders, trade associations, civic and community leaders, potential funders, and the media.

Messages

Shaping messages that matter to audiences and moving them to take action is harder than ever. Every day, we are bombarded by thousands of messages. Emails. Faxes. Texts. Ads. And now, tweets! In the social media age, audiences are not passive slugs sitting on a couch waiting for someone to send them an impersonal message.

Today's audiences want to be actively engaged in the communications process. So crafting messages that not only cut through the clutter, but also connect on a more personal level work best. Nonprofit audiences are really stakeholders who want a chance to think, respond, and be part of the conversation.

With good audience insights, you can successfully develop a compelling message platform that will resonate with stakeholders, whether delivery involves story telling, content sharing, humor, metaphors, or traditional dissemination.

The art and science of message development is complex and requires rewarding the audience with something they need or want. It must connect on an emotional, cultural, and personal level to be most effective. Later in this book, read "Shaping Messages that Stick" and "Multicultural Communications for Nonprofits" in "Part III: Nonprofit Communications: Let's Talk" to learn how to resonate with audiences.

Communications Channels

In today's Web 2.0 environment, more communications channels are available than ever before to exchange messages, share information, and build dialogues. Communications channels are the mediums and methods used to engage audiences. To select the most effective channels for your nonprofit, first take an inventory of every medium used.

Are your channels getting the job done? Is your organization missing opportunities to communicate with audiences? What mediums are your stakeholders using, including news and social media, and what might be a good fit for your organization? You can gather your own research through online surveys and interviews or turn to the latest media usability data available through Arbitron, The Nielsen Company, Vocus, Pew Internet & American Life Project, and the American Press Institute, among others.

Below are communications channels widely used today.

- Digital media.
- Social media and blogs.
- Print and broadcast media.
- Mobile.
- Print materials.
- Advertising.
- Word of mouth.
- Special events.

These mediums and many other channels offer your nonprofit a chance to communicate with stakeholders in multiple ways.

Tactics

Tactics are the wheels that make your communications plan go. If you select the right tactics, you'll reach your destination, achieving your strategy, goals, and objectives. Your budget and resources, of course, drive tactics. Choosing the most effective communications channels and approach for each tactic will be critical to success. When planning tactics, don't forget to think carefully about timing and priorities.

Examples of communications tactics that are often used by nonprofits include:

- Design or redesign a website.
- Create a social media network.
- Conduct a media outreach campaign.
- Create bi-lingual publications.
- Develop marketing templates.
- Deliver presentations and media training.
- Identify and promote spokespersons.
- Attend conferences and forums.
- Write success stories.

Budget

Budgeting and staffing present the toughest challenges for nonprofits with limited resources. You'll need to ask some hard questions to determine whether you have the in-house capacity to implement your communications plan, or if you need outside assistance, or require additional funding sources.

Will you need to phase in the communications plan over multiple years? This is why it's important to think about your available budget and staffing while you are planning strategy and tactics.

Evaluation

Nonprofits and government agencies are under increasing pressure to account for spending with measureable results. How can we do more with less? Are we making progress toward our goals and objectives and is communications advancing our mission? Is what we're doing and saying working and what is our return on investment? These are the hard questions you may be asked to justify your communications plan.

So think carefully about ways you can track and evaluate outcomes as part of your communications plan – whether it involves online surveys, metrics, web analytics, media monitoring, or follow-up interviews. Make sure your plan is about performance. Management and funders will love you when you can provide hard evidence that communications is making a difference.

Social Marketing: The Science of Behavior Change

Buckle up. Stop smoking. Don't pollute. Exercise regularly. Welcome to the world of social marketing, the science of behavior change. Social marketing is a complex discipline with a sole purpose, getting an individual or community to modify their behavior for social good.

Change isn't always easy and neither is social marketing. In fact, it can be downright frustrating and measurable results can be slow to achieve. Think marathon, not a 10K race. How do you convince people to voluntarily adopt a positive behavior that actually sticks?

Social marketing came of age in the 1970s and is often misunderstood and mistaken for social media marketing in today's Web 2.0 environment. Social marketing brings together the use of social and behavioral sciences (like sociology, anthropology, and psychology) with marketing strategies and tactics used by the commercial and public sectors.

Give and Get In Return

To work effectively, social marketing must involve an exchange or mutual benefit. If I give something, what do I get in return? This concept is rooted in commercial marketing. Give me two bucks, and I will give you a bottle of Gatorade that comes with hydration benefits, along with the emotional brand rewards associated with the popular sports drink.

The social marketing motive, in contrast, is not profit but instead change to benefit society. And just as consumers have choices, your audience can do something else, too. Your audience may decide to adopt another behavior. You want your audience to read, but they choose to play video games or watch television.

Social marketing practitioners are change agents. They are dedicated to important social issues and causes that result in positive behavior modification and improved outcomes, whether it's preventing injuries or saving lives. They are committed to the cause, not just to the creation of a new advertising campaign or logo.

In the Beginning

With the publication of *"Social Marketing: An Approach to Planned Social Change"* by Philip Kotler and Gerald Zaltman, social marketing became a formal discipline in 1971. Other researchers and practitioners, including Alan Andreasen, Bill Novelli, and Bill Smith, have advanced social marketing over the past three decades.

Today, social marketing's influence and reach are profound. Many government and nonprofit social marketing campaigns have had a powerful impact on public health, safety, education, and the environment. Social marketing courses are taught at major universities today, including Georgetown University.

Social Marketing Issues

Social marketing has been used to address many social issues, including:

- Domestic violence.
- Drug abuse.
- Smoking.
- Energy conservation.
- Obesity.
- Oral health.
- Recycling.
- Suicide.
- Teen pregnancy.

The list goes on. And so do the many ways practitioners seek to apply social marketing principles and social policy approaches to today's diverse social challenges.

Defining Social Marketing

Definitions for social marketing have evolved. Two widespread ones are:

"Social marketing is a process that applies marketing principles and techniques to create, communicate and deliver value in order to influence target audience behaviors that benefit society as well as the target audience." (Philip Kotler, Nancy Lee, and Michael Rothschild, 2006)

"Social marketing is a process for creating, communicating and delivering benefits that a target audience(s) wants in exchange for audience behavior that benefits society without financial profit to the marketer." (Bill Smith, 2006)

Campaigns for Change

Two of my favorite campaigns are "Click It or Ticket" (National Highway Traffic Safety Administration (NHTSA) and Go Red for Women (American Heart Association.) Click It or Ticket was designed to increase the use of seat belts among young people in the United States, while Go Red for Women empowers women to take charge of their heart health.

Heart disease is the number one killer of women in the United States. The use of red solidifies the cause, resonates with women, and reinforces the American Heart Association's brand identity.

Who can forget the famous USDA Forest Service mascots Smokey Bear (Only You Can Prevent Forest Fires) and Woodsy Owl (Give a Hoot – Don't Pollute). I was a kid when the late Harold Bell created Woodsy Owl in time for the first Earth Day in 1970. Woodsy is still around today and his latest motto is "Lend a Hand – Care for the Land!"

Back in college, I remember a journalism professor making me write "Smokey Bear" 50 times because I incorrectly thought the Associated Press style was "Smokey the Bear." According to the Ad Council, Smokey Bear's message is recognized by 95% of adults and 77% of children in the United States. In 2001, the message was updated to "Only You Can Prevent Wildfires." Smokey and Woodsy have been social marketing icons for a long time and convinced many of us to "do the right thing" for the environment.

Back in the early 1990s, while working at the Interstate Truckload Carriers Conference (now the Truckload Carriers Association), I got my first taste of social marketing, helping to plan and implement a campaign working in conjunction with Mothers Against Drunk Driving (MADD).

We launched a national highway safety awareness tour, "Drunk Driving Destroys Dreams," and held "rolling press conferences" in cities across the country. More than 130,000 red ribbons were distributed to the public and displayed on trucks. Millions of media impressions were generated with help from celebrities and professional athletes. An 18-wheeler displaying our campaign theme was seen by thousands as we moved along major interstates and interior routes.

Our goal was to curb drunk driving during the holidays and increase highway safety awareness. Local schools, law enforcement, and governments supported the campaign as well. At one press conference, Crash-Test Dummies Vince and Larry joined us. In 2010, NHTSA donated the famous dummies to Smithsonian's National Museum of American History after they promoted seat belt usage for nearly 25 years.

In 2010, I worked closely with Equals Three Communications in Bethesda, Maryland and the Metropolitan Washington Council of Governments to plan and implement a regional diesel idle reduction campaign, "Avoid the Fine, Don't Idle." The social marketing campaign was designed to encourage bus and truck drivers to reduce idling and promote public health. All these examples highlight how nonprofits and government, sometimes working with partners, engage social marketing principles for social good.

Five Phases of a Social Marketing Campaign

Different approaches and strategies have been used to achieve social marketing success.

Here are five campaign phases to consider.

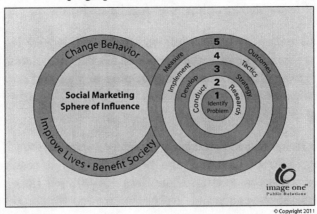

© Copyright 2011

Phase I: Identify the Problem

Before you embark on a social marketing campaign, you need to identify the problem. What is your rationale and need for conducting a change campaign? For example, your community has a high incidence of obesity. A social marketing campaign may help to combat this health issue, but you need to ask questions, gather data, and analyze. Get the big picture and an understanding on several levels, from the community down to the individual. Once the problem has been identified and clearly stated, you can begin the formative research phase, which will help you to fill in critical information gaps and gain better insights about your target audience(s).

Phase II: Conduct Research

The research phase is critical to campaign success. It's here where you will find out your target audience's attitudes, motivations, and behaviors. Research can also determine the characteristics of your audience and how to segment them into more homogeneous groups for better responsiveness to your campaign. Research will also help you learn about potential barriers to behavioral modification and your audience's readiness to change. Research is also conducted at the end of the campaign (evaluation) and to pre-test messages. It may also be needed during the campaign to test messages and materials and refine your approach.

Research will be used to align your strategy, goal, objectives, and tactics with your audience's needs and wants and how to satisfy them. Audience needs versus wants may vary widely. Research may involve quantitative, qualitative, or secondary research and include literature reviews, online surveys, focus groups, personal/telephone interviews and analysis of new and existing data. A SWOT (strengths, weaknesses, opportunities, and threats) analysis can help you to determine internal and external factors that could impact campaign success.

In some cases, research may involve monitoring and observation to gain a deeper understanding of your audience in their natural environment. For example, as part of our research for the diesel idle reduction campaign, I went out to a truck stop in Maryland and interviewed drivers as they were coming in. I also observed the idling habits of bus and truck drivers at different locations. The stronger your research efforts, the better chances the campaign will resonate with stakeholders. Research will help answer the question whether old behavior can be abandoned and new behavior adopted.

Phase III: Develop Strategy

The strategy phase brings together all you have learned to create an integrated communications plan and marketing mix (the Four Ps) that will strike a responsive chord with your audience(s). The key to this stage is establishing a realistic goal, objectives, and tactics based on your budget and the audience's ability to modify their behavior.

Developing messages that move your audience to take action is paramount to success. Answer the question: How will we get the audience to change? Social marketing practitioners often use the "Four Ps of Marketing" to develop the basis for their outreach strategy.

The four Ps (Kotler and Lee) are Product, Price, Place, and Promotion. The four Ps have been used in commercial marketing for decades and are often applied to social marketing principles. Sometimes a fifth P (Policy) is used, especially in public health campaigns. Advancing public policy through grassroots outreach, legislation, or the media can lead to new laws or funding that can positively impact behavior change at the community and individual levels.

The Four Ps of Social Marketing

Product – The behavior you intend to achieve and how you make it happen. It's "packaging" or "selling" the social modification in ways that meet the wants, needs, and desires of the target audience. So perhaps it's an education campaign, a poster contest, or a tangible product (such as a book about eating properly and exercising regularly) that motivates the audience to accept your message and change their behavior. It can also be intangible and tied to emotions, such as feeling safe or happy for contributing to a good cause like improving the environment. Because you are marketing a product, a positioning statement will be useful.

Price – The cost to make the behavior change, including money, recognition, time, and inconvenience. The price may be incentives (such as coupons or bonuses) or it may have negative consequences, such as fines and social stigma.

Place – Where the behavior change needs to take place. It's also the location campaign materials (products) are presented to the audience or where it's on their minds. It could be at home, a hotline, a mall, a clinic, a school, church, or hundreds of other places where your target audience will be most receptive to your message.

Promotion – The messages and communications channels used in the campaign to bring about the desired behavioral change. It includes the messengers for the campaign, such as spokespersons, partners, and media. Promotion often involves an integrated communications platform with use of advertising, public service announcements, public relations, social media, and direct mail. It may also include promotional items, coupons, and special events.

Phase IV: Implement Tactics

With a well-researched strategy and plan in place, it's time to implement the tactics. Implementation works toward achieving your objectives and ultimately your goal to change behavior. It's sticking to a time schedule and putting your tactics and marketing mix into action. It's writing the news releases, preparing and giving speeches, posting blogs, putting up posters, building the website, calling reporters, staffing the hotline, placing ads, and distributing t-shirts.

Phase V: Measure Outcomes

So how well did your campaign work? Did it actually change behavior in the community or target audience? Evaluation and monitoring instruments, whether these are follow-up surveys, interviews, or data collection, are essential to determine if your campaign worked, is working, or needs adjusting. Evaluation should track whether your objectives were met and how much they contributed toward achievement of your goal. Campaign impact and outcomes can also be measured through statistical comparisons – before and after the campaign.

Social marketing is not for everyone. It's a challenging undertaking and an important marketing discipline that will continue to evolve as our environment, needs, and wants change. It has a tremendous capacity to inspire good, improve lives, and change communities.

Cause Marketing for Social Good

Cause marketing presents nonprofits with exciting opportunities to expand their reach and capacity to fundraise through the powerful arms of corporate branding and marketing. At the heart of cause marketing or cause-related marketing (CRM) are mutually beneficial relationships between a nonprofit and a corporation.

Effective cause marketing is a win-win for both the nonprofit and the corporation as they pool resources and blend strategies to:

- Promote good causes.
- Build brand equity.
- Connect with stakeholders, including consumers, employees, and supporters.
- Share a meaningful message.

Consumer behavior studies, such as those conducted by Cone/ Duke University, confirm that Americans have a more positive image of a product or company when it supports a cause they care about. It's clear that cause marketing can drive consumer choice and raise awareness across diverse issues that impact us every day – issues such as health, education, and the environment.

Big Companies, Just Causes

Businesses often tie their cause marketing to corporate responsibility initiatives. Although companies have been practicing cause-marketing principles for more than a century, American Express introduced the cause-related marketing term in 1983 when it launched a CRM effort that raised $1.7 million for the preservation of the Statue of Liberty and Ellis Island. American Express donated one cent to the restoration every time someone used its charge card and $1 for each new card issued.

According to American Express, the company has supported important causes since the 1850s when employees contributed to the fundraising effort to build a pedestal for the Statue of Liberty, making it not only a symbol of opportunity, but also an icon of cause-related marketing.

The fight against cancer has been the focus of several highly influential and successful cause-marketing campaigns, including the Nike LIVESTRONG Bracelet, Lee National Denim Day, and Yoplait Save Lids to Save Lives.

Nike LIVESTRONG® Bracelets – Nike partnered with the Lance Armstrong Foundation in 2004 to raise funds and awareness for the champion cyclist's cancer charity and the LIVESTRONG brand has taken off ever since. To date, the iconic yellow rubber bracelets have generated more than $70 million for the Lance Armstrong Foundation. The gender-neutral campaign has used sport as a powerful tool for social good.

In 2010, while training for the Pittsburgh Marathon, I became part of the LIVESTRONG phenomenon, raising $965.00 in the war against cancer in memory of my parents who died of the disease. During the race, I proudly wore my yellow Nike Team LIVESTRONG shirt and hat. LIVESTRONG provides participants with a personalized fundraising site and tools, along with one-to-one support from staff.

Lee National Denim Day® – Lee Jeans kicked off this special day in 1996 and it has had a remarkable impact. The idea started when Lee employees realized each of them had somehow been affected by breast cancer. According to Lee Jeans, the company set a first-year goal of raising $1 million on Lee National Denim Day. To achieve this, Lee Jeans invited companies to go causal for a cause, inviting employees to wear their jeans to work on Denim Day in exchange for a $5 contribution to the fight against breast cancer.

Since its first year, Lee National Denim Day has raised more than $83 million and has brought together men and women to support an important cause. Celebrity spokespersons have included such notables as Pierce Bronson, Christina Applegate, Lucy Lui, Tim Daly, and Rob Lowe.

Yoplait Save Lids to Save Lives® – Millions of consumers have mailed in pink yogurt lids to raise 10 cents to support Susan G. Komen for the Cure®. Since 1998, this inspiring cause marketing campaign has raised more than $25 million in the battle against breast cancer.

All of these cause-marketing efforts and many more reflect rewarding partnerships that inspire good. They also demonstrate a strong interest by individuals to do something worthwhile.

Cause marketing is not just for large corporations and big nonprofits. Smaller businesses and nonprofits can jump into the game with the right partners and marketing strategy. Nonprofits thinking about entering the cause-marketing arena should ask the following questions:

1. What cause matches our mission?
2. Which corporate partner aligns best with our values and mission?
3. What mutual benefits will we and our corporate partner share by forming a cause-marketing relationship?

In creating an effective cause-marketing campaign, consider the following planning tips:

- Do your homework to determine the feasibility of your cause campaign and its potential to do social good.
- Define and understand your target audience through formative research.
- Develop a cause-marketing plan that includes a goal, objectives, expected outcomes, budget, timeline, and evaluation.
- Define the non-profit-corporate relationship, roles, and responsibilities.
- Create a joint marketing, public relations, and advertising plan.

By crafting a clear vision and plan for your cause-marketing campaign, you will be better positioned to connect with your target audience in meaningful ways that maximize success.

Micromarketing in the Mini Cooper Age

Mass marketing and Model Ts are out. Micromarketing and Mini Coopers are in. Today, as the social media influence rages on and communications channels multiply, successful marketing grows more targeted than ever.

A fundamental switch from mass to micromarketing is being driven by new technologies, an overcrowded marketplace, fragmented media, and cluttered minds. Thousands of new products enter the U.S. market each year, joining a bulging portfolio of brands. Micromarketing, which emerged in the early 1990s, is fueled by growing consumer demand for customized goods and services, along with increased opportunities to engage in brand conversations through social media.

When television first exploded onto the American scene six decades ago, brands were brought right into our living rooms. It was often Geritol, Kraft, and Coca Cola in the single-sponsor era of the 1950s. Advertising switched to a mass-merchandising concept in the 1960s and brands, such as Tide, Crest, and Charmin, became household names in the golden age of television. In those days, a few brand names were the norm.

Millions of Brands

Today, there are too many messages and brands, and it has caused a traffic jam in our minds. Kantar Media tracks approximately 3 million brands. With such a proliferation of new brands, our brains are blocking out mass advertising.

Other complex factors are contributing to the micromarketing boom. America today is much more diverse and consumers want tailored products that fit particular needs and tastes. The one-size fits-all product has lost its impact. Consumers in the micromarketing era want to be special.

Narrowly Defined Markets

Enter micromarketing. Instead of focusing on a vast sea of consumers, micromarketing uses demographics and other research to target specific market segments. At its best, micromarketing strikes a responsive chord with a narrowly defined market segment.

For example, BMW's Mini Cooper aims to draw young affluent drivers and older Mini enthusiasts. BMW latched on to the retro image – much like Volkswagen's New Beetle. And now, the Chevy Volt, Nissan Leaf, and 2012 Ford Focus are designed to connect with environmentally conscious consumers ready to make the leap to electric cars.

Hot technology brands, such as iPads, iPhones, Blackberrys, and Bluetooth, are being promoted through micromarketing. There are even iPods for Mini Coopers. Tomorrow, another wave of brands will become pop culture icons – thanks to micromarketing.

With new metrics, analytics, and market research methods, we know a lot more about consumers today, whether it's moms with kids at home, tweens, teens, boomers, or the responsible generation. Ethnic consumers, too, hold powerful purchasing power. Big companies with big brands are zooming in on individual preferences.

In 2010, for example, PUMA launched a Creative Factory for iPad to offer in-store customization and co-creation with the sports shoemaker brand. Customers build their own shoes with materials from PUMA and complete their design on the iPad. The order is sent to a factory for assembly. It's micromarketing at its finest.

Marketing on Consumer's Terms

In a noisy marketplace, it makes economic sense to focus more on micromarketing. There are so many new creative and affordable options today that provide marketers and advertisers with greater opportunities to reach consumers in their everyday environment and on their own terms.

Applications, microblogging, videosharing, podcasts, web portals, and social media take micromarketing to a new level and cost far less than mass marketing and advertising campaigns. Traditional media, too, offer increased micromarketing venues.

Today, there are more than 100 major cable channels, most of which target specific market segments, and more than 13,000 radio stations in the United States. Magazines remain a vital medium for micromessaging. Many new magazines are geared toward readers with special interests. Newspapers, the oldest mass medium, are adapting to micromarketing with targeted online publications and special editions that meet specific reader needs. Ethnic media present many opportunities to do micromarketing. Campus newspapers offer an excellent micromarketing channel to reach college students.

Since 1990, micromarketing has bombarded sports arenas with digital billboards. Corporations spend large sums to have their names put on sport stadiums – in what is both mass and micromarketing. Instant messaging, mobile websites, and cell phones, via text messages, are growing micromarketing platforms.

Today's savvy consumers like to be in control and will zap unwanted marketing in a nano-second. Although mass marketing will probably never die completely, it is taking a backseat to the world of micromarketing.

Nonprofit organizations should not be afraid to take the plunge. Knowing your audiences, their tastes, needs, and wants should drive your micromarketing strategies. In the age of social media and Mini Coopers, the future looks bright for micromarketing. The horizon is filled with dynamic mediums that can connect with consumers on a personal level.

Chapter 3

Your Nonprofit Playbook

"No one is useless in the world who lightens the burden of it for anyone."
– Charles Dickens

The best nonprofits run like well-oiled business machines. It may seem cold and commercial, but it's true. Nonprofits that take a few pages from the corporate playbook can go far. Behaving like a business makes perfect sense for nonprofits that must compete for funding and resources in a hyper-competitive climate.

Both corporations and nonprofits are mission driven with a bottom line to meet for survival. And while companies are focused on staying close to customers, nonprofits are centered on connecting with stakeholders and service recipients.

Here are seven communications strategies that can help your nonprofit accelerate success.

1) Be a Sponge.
2) Seize Opportunities.
3) Build Strategic Alliances.
4) Start Conversations.
5) Embrace Change.
6) Put Technology to Work.
7) Invest in Excellence.

These seven strategies are rooted in business theory, but are crafted in not-for-profit practice. The strategies may serve Fortune 500 companies well, but they are meant for the soup kitchen around the corner. Think like a business. Succeed like a nonprofit should.

1. Be a Sponge

Do you know how Abraham Lincoln became a great leader who united us and healed our nation's wounds? He became a sponge. And so should your nonprofit. Honest Abe was an avid reader who absorbed knowledge. He was also a conversationalist and storyteller. Above all, he listened and stayed in touch with the everyday citizen. He knew how to make the connection. Lincoln believed in the "better angels of our nature."

Lincoln always kept an ear to the ground, gathering intelligence and learning new strategies and tactics that advanced his administration's goals for the betterment of the country. He leveraged it all to build support, mobilize people, and inspire action. Today, nearly 150 years after Lincoln's death, his lifelong learning and listening habits hold value for nonprofits.

Listen and Learn

Your nonprofit can learn a lot by listening to stakeholders within and outside the organization. And by absorbing information about hot trends affecting your organization and the independent sector, your nonprofit will be better positioned to meet challenges and stay on the cutting edge.

By listening, you will increase trust and gain a better understanding of what stakeholders and supporters are saying about your nonprofit. You can then design more effective communications and marketing strategies that reflect audience needs and wants, while keeping your nonprofit current with the times.

Here are five primary ways you can collect both quantitative and qualitative research that will aid your nonprofit in gaining deeper audience understanding. Think of these as listening tools that engage stakeholders, including donors, funders, members, volunteers, partners, and service recipients.

Annual Survey

Conducting an annual survey is an excellent instrument for listening and collecting valuable insights from stakeholders. This online instrument presents an opportunity to engage stakeholders, gather data, and get a pulse on current perceptions. Ask critical questions about what issues are important and relevant. Which communications products and services work best or need refining? How can we encourage conversation and build dialogue? Are our communications channels working? How do stakeholders feel about our brand and what level of visibility do we have?

[handwritten margin note: pre work questionnaire]

Focus Groups

To gather qualitative input, try conducting focus groups that bring together stakeholders in an informal discussion. You'll need a good facilitator who understands the dynamics of your organization and a series of questions to ask participants. Keep the size manageable at up to 12 participants per session. Ideally, try to keep the time frame to two hours and offer food and refreshments.

Focus groups can help you dig deeper into issues and perceptions about your nonprofit and its communications function. Encourage broad participation reflective of your stakeholders and have someone take accurate notes. Conclude your focus group with a short five or six question survey that touches on the questions asked during the session, giving participants a final opportunity to express their opinions separate from the group.

Website Analytics *[handwritten: — become better versed]*

Your website can tell you how stakeholders are interacting with your organization and to what degree. Web analytics measure traffic to sites and can be used as a tool for evaluating campaigns and optimizing web usage. By tracking hits, page views, and visits, you can determine what content stakeholders are most interested in, giving you valuable information for improving communications performance.

Social Media Monitoring

You can also uncover conversations and potential influencers by monitoring blogs and social media. By engaging with your own stakeholders through your nonprofit's social media channels and by analyzing and participating in the conversations, you are listening and engaging your brand. For more sophisticated and targeted monitoring, you can turn to vendors such as Vocus, which use social media software to track social media activity.

I know more about this?

Media Tracking

If you want to gauge how your nonprofit is portrayed by the media or if you want to monitor news coverage about a relevant issue, media tracking is the right tool. Some nonprofits subscribe to clipping and news monitoring services, such as LuceBurrelles, or sign up to receive Google News Alerts. You will need to build a list of key word searches relevant to your organization.

Keep a log of media coverage that specifically notes your organization and analyze it for impact. Some organizations track the number of earned media impressions gained, which is the number of potential readers, viewers, or listeners exposed to your message. By analyzing news coverage, you can also track polls and other trends that have meaning for your organization and its stakeholders.

Absorb and Advance

In addition to listening, it's important to absorb as much information as you can about new trends, techniques, and fresh ideas that can enhance your communications skills and your organization's capacity to connect with stakeholders in meaningful ways.

For 17 years, during my undergraduate, graduate, and early professional years, I always worked part-time at a bookstore. It was a whole education in itself and I found out you can learn a lot just by keeping an eye on the bestseller lists to track what's hot and what's not. Every year, hundreds of new marketing and nonprofit books are published. You can't read them all but it's good to stay abreast as much as possible.

Subscribing to publications and associations that are relevant to communications and your nonprofit will help you to sharpen your skills and enhance organizational performance. *The Chronicle of Philanthropy*, *The NonProfit Times*, and *Nonprofit Quarterly* are valuable information sources for nonprofit professionals. Consider joining your state association for nonprofits.

Several large national membership organizations also support communications professionals at the national and local levels, including:

- American Institute of Graphic Arts (AIGA)
- ASAE (The Center for Association Leadership)
- Association of Fundraising Professionals, (AFP)
- The American Marketing Association (AMA)
- The International Association of Business Communicators (IABC)
- The Public Relations Society of America (PRSA)

2. Seize Opportunities

You never know when the next big opportunity will knock. When it does, open the door! In 2006, while waiting for a flight to Florida to deliver a workshop on nonprofit marketing for a government client, I saw Hall of Fame Pitcher Jim Palmer sitting alone at the next gate. I seized the opportunity. I grew up a big Baltimore Orioles fan and just had to meet one of my boyhood sports idols. Palmer was wonderful. We talked a little baseball. He wished me good luck with the session, and I was on my way. What a moment!

Later that year, I made "seizing opportunities" a focal point during a marketing session for Neighborhood Networks centers. The U.S. Department of Housing and Urban Development (HUD) created Neighborhood Networks in 1995 to help bridge the digital divide by establishing computer technology centers in low-income housing communities. I had the pleasure of co-presenting the session, "Fundraising: Beyond the Basics," with Network for Good CEO Bill Strathmann.

The point is opportunities will sometimes appear out of nowhere. Sure, we constantly strive to create opportunities, but occasionally they pop up unexpected. Don't let them pass you by. What if, for example, *ABC World News Tonight* just called and wanted to include your nonprofit in a feature story. This actually happened to Lutheran Services in America (LSA) when we were publicizing the nonprofit's online auction, Trading Graces. The story angle focused on "regifting" during the holidays and LSA President Jill Schumann seized the opportunity to gain national attention for her organization. Schumann gave a great interview and the media exposure helped the cause and strengthened the nonprofit's visibility.

Opportunities may present themselves in different ways and at unexpected times. Maybe it's a new partnership opportunity that puts your organization on the map. It could be inclusion in a documentary or a book. Or you may be asked to speak at a conference or submit a white paper on a timely topic.

Take advantage of opportunities as they come, especially when they don't cost anything, except time well spent. The window often shuts quickly. So don't hesitate. Act fast!

3. Build Strategic Alliances

Building alliances or strategic partnerships can give your nonprofit a boost, whether it's a media sponsorship that expands communications channels or a local business that opens up new markets for your organization. Strategic alliances bring together two or more organizations to maximize human and financial resources. In forming an alliance, nonprofits may choose to work with other nonprofits, government agencies, or businesses that share a common interest.

Strong alliances can help your nonprofit to:

- Overcome challenges and advance your mission.
- Gain a competitive advantage in pursuing grants.
- Extend your brand and increase visibility.
- Connect with target audiences.

Successful alliances are built on good fits where both partners share a vision and receive benefit from collaboration. For example, Volunteers of America partners with The Major League Baseball Players Trust to promote the nurturing and well-being of America's children and their families. The partnership features the personal involvement of major league baseball players and their families with a variety of programs conducted by Volunteers of America throughout the United States.

Also together, Volunteers of America and The Major League Baseball Players Trust administer Action Team, a national youth volunteer program inspiring the next generation of volunteers across the United States. According to Volunteers of America, Action Teams across the country have inspired more than 25,000 high school students to help over 100,000 people in need by helping in the community.

In 2009, Boy Scouts of America and Minor League Baseball teamed up with the Federal Emergency Management Agency

(FEMA) to help families prepare for emergencies. In partnership with FEMA's *Ready Campaign*, dozens of local Boy Scout councils and baseball teams stepped up to the plate and encouraged fans to prepare for all types of emergencies and disasters. The *Ready Campaign* is a national public awareness effort designed to help Americans prepare their families before the next emergency or disaster by making a kit and getting a plan.

While working for Kauffman & Associates, Inc. in 2010, I was fortunate to help test messaging and communications concepts as part of focus groups conducted in Alaska and New Mexico. The communications research with Native American audiences was in preparation for a *Ready Campaign* launch in Indian Country.

Through a partnership between Boys & Girls Clubs of America and the Environmental Protection Agency's (EPA) ENERGY STAR program, thousands of youth are learning how to reduce energy use and lower energy bills at home and in the community. The ENERGY STAR hero campaign includes national advertising.

Clearly, effective strategic alliances are all about win-win relationships. But your nonprofit has to be ready to enter into an alliance and it must remain active and committed. So the partner assessment stage is critical. You need to feel comfortable with the collaboration and your mutual responsibilities. Working with the right partner, you can achieve so much more.

4. Start Conversations

In 2011, *"The Social Network"* captured three Academy Awards. The popular film tells the riveting story of how Mark Zuckerberg started Facebook and played a primary role in the launch of the social media movement as we know it today. In 2011, America also observed the 100th birthday of former President Ronald Reagan, who was called the "Great Communicator." Reagan, a one-time actor, was known for his ability to articulate his political vision and connect with the American people.

But we often ignore, arguably, one of the most influential conversation starters of all – Marshall McLuhan, a famed communications theorist who coined the terms the "Global Village" and the "Medium is the Message." In 2011, we also commemorate 100 years of McLuhan, whose prediction that technology would turn the world into a Global Village is in many ways a worldwide reality today. I remember reading about McLuhan in journalism school at the University of Maryland and how he envisioned an electronic community with no borders. McLuhan, whose vintage book, *Understanding Media: The Extensions of Man*, came of age during the apocalyptic 1960s, is relevant once again.

Nearly four decades later, more than ever before, nonprofits and their stakeholders have powerful tools and communications channels for starting conversations and sharing their voices. Whether it's a blog, online groups, Facebook, or Twitter, the social media movement has widened the street for communicators seeking immediate feedback and participation from audiences.

Nonprofits that are listening and responding to stakeholders are gaining valuable insights that enhance their communications by:

- Increasing understanding.
- Shaping perceptions.
- Raising visibility.
- Extending the brand.
- Building lasting relationships.

By moving from monologues to dialogues, nonprofits can increase participation that can attract potential volunteers, increase donors, broaden support, engage influencers, and inspire meaningful outcomes.

Social media is not the only game in town. More traditional strategies and venues for starting conversations include open houses, attending conferences, exhibiting, hosting an information line, exchanging ideas at meetings, and going directly to stakeholders.

With the rapid rise of social media, combined with the ancient art of telling stories and creative expression, the sky is the limit for nonprofits interested in building meaningful and lasting relationships with stakeholders.

5. Embrace Change

Remember the Dr. Seuss story about the North-Going Zax and the South-Going Zax who refused to budge in their tracks for 59 years. A highway was build right over the two stubborn Zax and the world moved on without them. Time did not stand still.

We can't stop progress. We must adapt and remain flexible or the world and competition will pass us by. Nonprofits need foresight and so do we as communications professionals. New and social media have dramatically changed our roles as communicators and we must welcome it. Nonprofits, too, that loathe change will be left behind. They'll be stuck in the mud or digging their own graves.

In my view, two primary factors that impact change in nonprofits are fear of the unknown and tunnel vision. Nonprofits naturally run on tight, conservative operating budgets that leave little room for risk or trial and error. Why take a chance? But making positive changes can help your nonprofit to:

- Improve productivity.
- Enhance communications.
- Boost staff and volunteer performance.
- Reduce costs and eliminate waste.
- Deliver better services.

Change is good and well worth it when the outcomes can be measured. Unfortunately, many nonprofits are so stressed by internal dynamics, including insufficient staffing and limited resources, they can't make market adjustments fast enough. They stay focused on meeting daily challenges and fail to see shifts taking place. They miss opportunities and the big picture.

So how do we embrace change? Some nonprofits are forced to change in reaction to market conditions, economic realities, competition, technologies, and new regulations. Proactive nonprofits change on their own. They are committed to staying on the cutting edge. They chart a course for the future and are willing to take a few detours so long as they reach their destination.

Successful change, whether big or small, requires effective communication and executive support. How well your organization manages change can make all the difference. As your organization changes, make sure internal and external communication changes along with it.

6. Put Technology to Work

I love Macs. Maybe you don't. Perhaps you prefer reading books using Kindle. Give me a paperback instead. I like online giving, but you may still favor mailing in checks. But who can deny the role of technology in our daily lives and how it continues to evolve right before our very eyes.

Thirty years ago, while I was in journalism school at the University of Maryland, we still used typewriters. Today, those classrooms are loaded with the latest Apple Computers. In the late 1980s, while working for Aspen Publishers, Inc., we were thrilled to be part of the desktop publishing revolution. Using Aldus PageMaker, we worked on the early Macintosh Computers that looked like little TVs with inserts for floppy disks. It was so cool!

That same decade, while at the American Red Cross, we prepared newsletter copy using new word processing systems that expedited the entire editorial process. Fast forward to today and you'll find nonprofits using technology to do just about everything. Putting technology to work for your nonprofit can have a profound effect on your organization's success.

[Nonprofit communications professionals are using technology to distribute news, conduct e-mail marketing, perform online research, create e-newsletters, design annual reports, build websites, develop videos and podcasts, and monitor budgets. Nonprofits are increasingly engaging in mobile marketing, blogging, and social media. And just as fast as nonprofits adapt, new technologies emerge. It's a constant struggle to keep up.]

There is good news, however. Technology costs are more affordable today and many services are available through online vendors. For example, eTapestry offers accounting, database, website, and email marketing services for nonprofits. Think of technology as an investment. You should get much in return. By putting technology to work for your nonprofit, you will actually save money, streamline operations, and improve performance. Use technology to achieve specific communications goals and to advance your mission.

[Nonprofits seeking technology knowledge, resources, hot trends, and solutions can join TechSoup or The Nonprofit Technology Network (NTEN). These organizations are leaders in the nonprofit technology community committed to helping nonprofits use technology more effectively.]

 TechSoup.org (www.techsoup. org) is a project of TechSoup Global, a nonprofit worldwide network of individuals and organizations who believe that technology is a powerful enabler for social change. They've helped nonprofits and libraries to save more than $2 billion in IT expenses since 2001, with over 450 product donations from 44 partners (including Microsoft, Cisco, Symantec, and Adobe). They also provide free blog posts, articles, and webinars tailored to the needs of nonprofits.

NTEN (www.nten.org) connects members to each other, provides professional development opportunities, educates its constituency on issues of technology use in nonprofits, and spearheads groundbreaking research, advocacy, and education on technology issues. NTEN also publishes an annual Nonprofit Social Network Benchmark Report.

Armed with the right tools, knowledge, and the latest technology resources, your nonprofit will be well positioned for success now and in the future. Putting technology to work will streamline operations and advance your mission, while saving your organization time and money.) main pt.

7. Invest in Excellence

What is excellence and why should nonprofits invest in it? We have all achieved or experienced excellence. It's Beethoven's 5th Symphony. It's getting an A on a report card, a no hitter in baseball or a blue ribbon at the county fair. Excellence is a pair of running shoes that fit perfectly and pounds the pavements for hundreds of miles without wearing out. It's receiving customer service that leaves us smiling. Excellence moves beyond mediocrity and aims for greatness.

So what does excellence look like in a nonprofit and how is it achieved? Excellence in nonprofits may be exhibited many ways. Behind every successful nonprofit are talented and committed professionals and volunteers who are motivated to advance the mission.

In high-performing nonprofits, you'll also find the board of directors and executive management work in sync and share the same vision for the future. Excellence in nonprofits may also be demonstrated by effective work processes, solid accounting practices, and a focus on continuous improvement.

Effective and regular communications play a central role in driving organizational excellence, especially in the Web 2.0 environment. This is especially true for nonprofits that depend on communications to engage stakeholders and raise funds.

Not long ago, many nonprofit organizations thought of communications as a secondary function. Today, that perception still exists, but the far more frequent challenge is doing more with less. Common barriers facing nonprofit communications departments are limited budgets, a lack of resources, and insufficient staff. But don't despair. You can still achieve communications excellence by making smart choices and staying focused on quality.

Many nonprofits have an ingrained notion that the organization's website and marketing materials should not look "too good" to avoid appearing lavish to potential donors and funders. Rubbish! I believe just the opposite. I would argue that the better designed and attractive your communications; the more likely you will capture attention and inspire someone to take action.

First, you don't achieve excellence by striving for the ordinary. Second, the nonprofit marketplace is more competitive than ever and you need to be remarkable. Finally, many communications costs have actually dropped as a result of new technologies and economies of scale. So investing in excellence is more affordable.

For example, using Word Press, you can create a cutting-edge website for significantly less than many HTML websites. Today, many website templates have also been created that can easily be customized to fit your nonprofit's needs.

New content management systems allow you to make content changes quickly and easily. Printing costs, too, depending on the paper selection, have decreased with new digital technologies. And the cost difference in doing four-color printing versus two-color printing is indiscernible. So don't let concerns about costs and perceptions prevent you from creating quality communications products that connect with your stakeholders.

"Quality is a Habit"

Of course, quality is paramount to nonprofit and corporate success. You've heard the saying "You are only as good as your last..." In other words, quality is fleeting and you can never rest on your laurels. The history of the auto industry, for example, is rich with stories of quality defects, poor reliability, and recalls that damaged reputations and caused sales to plummet.

Think of the link between quality and reputation like this. Imagine a company that makes red balls fills a wire basket. But over time, you begin to see more and more yellow balls appear in the basket. Is it a red ball maker any more, or a lemon maker? You see the point.

As Aristotle noted, "Quality is not an act. It is a habit." Make quality control a priority at your nonprofit. Develop rigorous review and approval processes. Measure outcomes that will improve your organization's accountability to its many constituencies.

Compete for Awards C.D.

Finally, submit to communications and nonprofit awards that can increase visibility, reward staff performance, enhance credibility, and build your nonprofit's reputation for quality and excellence. Set aside an annual budget for award entries. Several distinguished marketing and communications awards include:

- APEX Awards for Publications Excellence (www.apexawards.com)
- Aurora Awards (multimedia) (www.auroraawards.com)
- Ava Awards (multimedia) (www.avaawards.com)
- Communicator Awards (www.communicatorawards.com)
- Hermes Creative Awards (www.hermesawards.com)

- IABC Silver Inkwell Awards (www.iabc.com/awards)
- MarCom Awards (www.marcomawards.com)
- PRSA Silver Anvil Awards (www.prsa.org/awards/silveranvil)
- Telly Awards (multimedia) (www.tellyawards.com)

Winning communications and nonprofit awards reinforces your organization's commitment to pursuing excellence. The statuettes on the shelves and certificates on the walls remind everyone that your nonprofit stands for quality and high performance.

Online Giving: The Network for Good Contribution

Network for Good. Online giving is rapidly changing the face of philanthropy and increasingly nonprofits are joining the high-tech fundraising trend. Nonprofits large and small are realizing the Internet's enormous potential.

A driving force behind the rise of online giving is Network for Good. Founded in 2001 by AOL, Yahoo!, and Cisco, Network for Good is the Internet's largest nonprofit giving resource. Based in Bethesda, Maryland, the nonprofit for nonprofits helped revolutionize the online giving process, raising more than $472 million in online donations for more than 60,000 nonprofit organizations.

Network for Good's mission is to make it easier for nonprofits to raise money online, and for people to give online. Network for Good developed an online donation processing service, called DonateNow, for nonprofits to accept credit card gifts on the Web. It also powers many social networks for social good and giving portals online.

Giving Still About Relationships

"Online giving has reached the tipping point," said Bill Strathmann, Chief Executive Officer, Network for Good. "Donors increasingly feel comfortable supporting charities in the comfort of their home or office. Like social media, online giving is a game changer for nonprofit organizations. But we are still learning and fundraising tools and technologies continue to evolve. We know that people who give online are no different than other donors in that they expect a relationship – not simply a transaction – with the organization they support."

The more intimate and emotionally coherent the giving experience, the stronger the relationship between donor and nonprofit appears to be, Strathmann said. In other words, online fundraising is all about relationships as it is in offline fundraising.

Cumulative donations through Network for Good yielded an average annual growth of 56 percent between 2003 and 2009, according to a Network for Good and True Sense Marketing survey. Sponsored by AOL, the study is available at www.onlinegivingstudy. org and covers $381 million in online giving through Network for Good's platform.

Since 2003, online giving has grown at a phenomenal rate, especially in the aftermath of hurricanes Katrina and Rita. Even during the economic downturn, online giving kept on going like the Energizer Bunny.

The annual Convio Online Marketing Benchmark Index Study, which evaluated results of nearly 600 nonprofit organizations, found that the median growth rate in online giving was 20 percent in 2010 despite a difficult economy. This compared to a median growth rate of 14 percent in 2009. Overall, 79 percent of organizations raised more in 2010 than in 2009. Meanwhile, total charitable giving by type of recipient is estimated to have increased by 3.8 percent in 2010, according to Giving USA 2011: The Annual Report on Philanthropy for the Year 2010. Giving USA Foundation (2011).

Online Giving Venues

Many charities use Network for Good as the giving engine behind their website. There are two ways this works:

1. A **charity branded giving page** is integrated with the charity's website. Other than the NetworkforGood.org URL, it's not evident that one has left the website to make a gift.
2. A **generic giving page** does not visually match the charity's website but goes to a Network for Good-branded multi-step checkout process that has the charity name and address to identify it.

Network for Good also powers social networks for social good, where donors can give to many charities and in many cases fundraise among their friends and family. Such sites include Causes on Facebook, Change.org, and YourCause.com. In addition, Network for Good powers giving portals, where donors can search and support any charity registered with the IRS. These include NetworkforGood.org, Guidestar.org, and CharityNavigator.org.

Fundraising with Foresight

The rise of social media, new applications, and advancing technologies will continue to fuel the growth and popularity of online giving. Speed. Flexibility. Cost effectiveness. Timeliness. These are the main advantages of engaging online giving. Electronic tracking also gives nonprofits an excellent tool for analyzing trends, products, and the effectiveness of fundraising campaigns.

How nonprofit organizations build relationships with donors and how they take advantage of the latest technologies are keys to successful fundraising today and in the future.

PART II

Building Brand Connections

Chapter 4

Brand Blazing and Beyond

All the world is full of suffering. It is also full of overcoming.
– Helen Keller

Nonprofit brands that connect with people on an emotional level can do amazing things. Like moving millionaires to give vast sums of their money away and getting kids to break their piggy banks to help others because it's the right thing to do. Powerful nonprofit brands can mobilize communities to save lives, convince corporations to write checks in the name of social responsibility, and persuade volunteers to generously commit their time and talents.

Successful branding can do all this and more. But can you actually put a value on your nonprofit brand? It's quite possible. The YMCA has the nation's most valuable nonprofit brand, worth an estimated $6.4 billion, according to Cone's 2009 Nonprofit Power Brand 100 study. The Salvation Army, the United Way, the American Red Cross, and Goodwill Industries round out the top five.

Today, nonprofit branding is not only art and science, but also a measure of financial performance and social significance in society. So how do you get stakeholders to see the light and find value in your unique mission? It all begins by building emotional connections with audiences and developing meaningful relationships built on trust.

Branding is about touching the heart by telling a great story visually and verbally. It's more than a logo, tagline, or colors. It's a total experience. Your nonprofit brand is not what you think it is, but how others perceive it. Branding truly is in the eye of the beholder. It's living up to a promise and putting a distinct stamp on your organization that separates it from the competition. Marketing expert Jack Trout sums it up well. "Differentiate or Die." The marketplace has simply become overcrowded with billions of brands and messages that bombard the brain.

To succeed, your nonprofit must be positioned in the mind of the target audience, whether it's a donor, partner, volunteer, or service recipient. For example, the American Red Cross is positioned as the leading disaster relief organization. A nonprofit does not have to be the leader in a particular field, but it should have a unique focus. You need to answer three important questions.

1) Why do we matter?
2) How do we become relevant?
3) How do we build a bond or connection with stakeholders?

Based on human cognitive systems, solving the branding mystery requires getting through filters in the brain that dismiss irrelevant information and tapping into personal experiences that hold meaning. Breaking through the clutter is not easy and you can't connect with everyone. With the right brand strategy, however, you can move the needle and win hearts over time.

Defining Branding

We've talked about branding and its potential impact. But how is it defined and what are its roots? Branding has been around for thousands of years. The ancient Greeks, Romans, and Egyptians branded pottery with symbols. Going back hundreds of years, branding refers to burning a mark into cattle to establish unique ownership.

Today, we still think of branding as creating a distinctive mark and a whole lot more. Branding is the sum of your best and worst products and services. It's defined by your organizations achievements and failures. It's a mirror image of perceptions from within and outside the organization. Branding is about getting your stakeholders to see you as the best and only choice. It's about creating fierce loyalty. Branding is the visual image, emotional appeal, and unique personality that you associate with a company, organization, or product.

Four Things Your Brand Must Do

Nonprofit brands that create space in the mind and build loyalty must do four things: 1) Earn Trust 2) Evoke Emotions 3) Stimulate the Senses and 4) Communicate Value.

1) Earn Trust

Earning trust is vital to successful branding. Stakeholders will accept or reject your brand if it does not live up to its promise. This is the driving success behind Allstate's "You're in good hands" slogan that has connected with consumers for more than 50 years. People want to know that they will be taken care of after an accident or when crisis strikes and a pair of hands add the perfect human touch. People must feel comfortable, too, knowing that your nonprofit will deliver on its mission.

A 2010 "Perspectives on Nonprofits" survey conducted by American Express revealed that 7 in 10 Americans (71%) trust nonprofits more than they trust government or industry to address some of the most pressing issues of our time. Nonprofits, for the most part, have earned our initial trust but it's not by accident. Trust is earned over time through integrity, truth, and a track record of success. Note that name recognition alone does not equate to trust. Open, honest, and consistent communications are essential to building trust. Good design, delivering quality, and a commitment to excellence also builds trust.

2) Evoke Emotions

Emotions play a powerful role in our brand decisions. Whether it's Coke, Apple, McDonalds, and Starbucks or national nonprofits, such as the American Cancer Society and the Make-a-Wish Foundation, top brands evoke an emotional attachment.

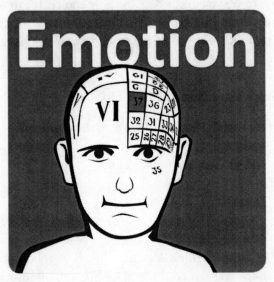

They tap into the human experience, including memories, and unconscious dreams. Brand design expert Marc Gobe calls it "emotional branding." Successful brands become a reference, a way of living, and a part of a person's daily life.

Nonprofit brands are woven into the American fabric. Every year, the Salvation Army appeals to our hearts in the spirit of the season with a united front of bell ringers and red kettles. In 2010, the nonprofit movement raised a record $142 million during its annual Red Kettle Christmas Campaign. And what about Girl Scout Cookies,® which have been part of our culture for generations?

Effective nonprofit brands inspire, comfort, engage, and even entertain us. They connect with us on a personal level, providing social and psychological benefits. They evoke intense emotions, whether it's hope, joy, love, laughter, pride, or confidence.

3) Stimulate the Senses

Brands come in many shapes, sizes, and scents and arouse the senses, which send data to the brain for processing and combine with stored messages from individual past experiences. For example, those Girl Scout Cookies® are delightful because they stimulate tiny taste buds in our tongue and mouth sending a message to our brain. Taste has been the focus of several legendary brand campaigns. For example, "Tastes great, less filling" (Miller Lite) and "Sorry Charlie. Starkist wants tuna that tastes good, not tuna with good taste."

For 100 years, Crayola crayons have combined color and smell to create an unforgettable experience. Yale University researchers tell us that the smell of crayons, along with coffee and peanut butter, are among the 20 most recognizable smells in the United States. Smell has the ability to trigger the memory, but sound is also a compelling tool for altering mood and product experiences. Who can forget the snack, crackle, and pop of Kellogg's Rice Krispies? Or the plop, plop, fizz, fizz of Alka-Seltzer. Touch is another strong sense that builds lasting brand connection. "Please don't squeeze the Charmin."

Nonprofits need to carefully consider how their brand touches the senses. Whether it's kettles, ringing bells, cookies, colors, songs, or packaging, nonprofits can enhance their brand power by tapping into emotions.

4) Communicate Value

Nonprofits are under increasing pressures to deliver value and demonstrate results. Saying you do good work is not enough. Donors and supporters demand measurable outcomes that show a solid return on social investment. How well your nonprofit communicates its value and success can have a big effect on brand perceptions.

Transparency and accountability are closely linked to trust. Nonprofits should openly and proactively share information about their mission, accomplishments, and finances. The information should be accessible on your website to increase public understanding and acceptance. Here branding moves beyond the intangible to the concrete and from the abstract to real.

All nonprofits can share impacts and benefits unique to their mission. It may be improving the quality of life, creating educational opportunities, a cost savings to society, strengthening the community, or preparing youth for tomorrow's workplace. The role of nonprofit communicators is to develop creative ways to show results. Measurable outcomes matter, and when combined with poignant success stories, send a powerful message.

For example, FoodLink for Tulare County highlights its value to the community next to a prominent *DONATE NOW* button on the nonprofit's website at www.foodlinktc.org. "For every $1 donated, FoodLink can provide $5 worth of food!" Now that's a hearty return on investment.

FoodLink for Tulare County, a Feeding America member, has earned a four-star Charity Navigator rating. Charity Navigator, America's premier independent charity evaluator, works to advance a more efficient and responsive philanthropic marketplace by evaluating the financial health of more than 5,500 of America's largest charities.

Based in California, FoodLink for Tulare County distributes approximately 7 million pounds of food annually. Through a network of more than 80 local nonprofit agencies, the nonprofit has been working to end hunger in Tulare County since 1978. In 2010, food distributed by FoodLink's efficient network of food collection, preservation, and distribution reached more than 120,000 people, with more than two thirds of those served being children.

Nonprofits like FoodLink that track and report measurable outcomes are in better position to boost their brand value and demonstrate their worth to the communities they serve. Communicating value gives nonprofits a competitive edge in their quest for funding, support, and long-term sustainability.

The Six Pillars of Branding

The influences of the ancient Greeks on modern civilization are profound. They helped lay the foundation for our government, the arts, language, math, science, philosophy, theater, and classic architecture. We marvel at the balance, symmetry, and simplicity of Greek architectural wonders that survive today.

One could argue that Aristotle and his work *"The Art of Rhetoric"* established the intellectual framework for branding as we know it today. The Greek philosopher theorized three primary ways to persuade audiences through communication: 1) Ethos (character) 2) Pathos (emotion) and 3) Logos (facts or reason). The Greeks, too, have inspired popular brand names, including Nike. And they serve as the thinking and blueprint behind the Six Pillars of Nonprofit Branding™.

The pillars are: 1) Research 2) Visualize 3) Verbalize 4) Promote 5) Protect and 6) Refine

Whether your nonprofit has not yet formed or has been "doing good" for more than a century, these basic building blocks can help your organization achieve brand success that stands the test of time.

The Six Pillars of Branding

R E S E A R C H — V I S U A L I Z E — V E R B A L I Z E — P R O M O T E — P R O T E C T — R E F I N E

Your Organization

Research

Brands are born, grow, and evolve, requiring research at different stages of development and management – including conception, naming, renaming, repositioning, and refinement. Research helps nonprofits to get a pulse on brand perceptions, attitudes, and awareness levels. It provides valuable intelligence on how to make your brand standout and resonate with target audiences in an overcrowded marketplace. Research also gives nonprofits an opportunity to listen and hold conversations with stakeholders that lead to better communication and stronger brand associations.

For nonprofits with limited communications staff and resources, research can be a scary word but discovering the essence of your brand does not have to drain your budget. A variety of quantitative and qualitative research methods and instruments, including online surveys, interviews, focus groups, secondary research, and evaluations, provide you with all the tools you need to define and refine your brand.

Conducting a brand audit, an independent review of your nonprofit's brand, provides an objective baseline for making sound strategic decisions. Brand audits are best performed by nonprofit marketing experts with knowledge of your mission. Effective brand audits determine how, when, and where stakeholders touch the brand.

They also:

- Identify stakeholders.
- Measure brand consistency.
- Gauge perceptions.
- Assess verbal and visual appeal.
- Analyze the competitive environment.
- Measure communications performance.

Typical brand research questions may include:

- What is it that we want to be known for in the marketplace? Is it quality, compassion, innovation, best value, cutting edge, fast delivery, or something else? Whatever you want to be known for, make sure you can live up to it.
- What are the tastes and needs of your stakeholders? Take a look at your audiences. What are their characteristics? What do they tell you about your nonprofit?
- When people see your nonprofit's name or logo, what do they think? What is their gut reaction?
- What are they saying about your organization?

When you have pulled together enough information from quantitative and qualitative research, complete a comprehensive analysis and weigh it carefully against what you know about your nonprofit and marketing communications to form a blueprint for your brand strategy.

Visualize

Thousands of years ago, hieroglyphics were used as a form of visual communication that blended logographic and alphabetic elements. The ancient Egyptian Eye of Horus symbol characterized the eye as a receptor of information containing six parts or doors to the senses (touch, taste, hearing, thought, sight, and smell). Today, thought is not one of the five primary senses.

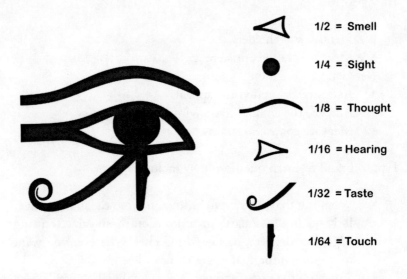

As communication increasingly moves online, our society becomes more visually dominant and dependent on symbols and icons. Inspiring design and imagery are aesthetic tools for tapping into our senses, creating a deeply satisfying brand experience. Images hold power over words. "Seeing is believing." This is especially true for brands that we instantly recognize by their visual identity. In 2011, for example, Starbucks unveiled a new logo with no words, leaving only the iconic mermaid. After 40 years, has the Starbucks brand simply outgrown words?

Compelling nonprofit brands, including the Salvation Army, the United Way, and Habitat for Humanity, still combine a strong visual identity with a striking message platform that work in harmony to create connections on a personal level.

The twin "V" pillars, Visualize and Verbalize, should complement each other to create the public face and voice of a nonprofit brand. A visual identity helps evoke emotions and adds brand meaning through design elements, including colors, shapes, symbols, and typography. Great design conveys the essence, personality, values, and culture of a brand to your target audiences.

When creating or refreshing a visual identity, remember to:

- Be memorable.
- Apply consistently.
- Touch all communication points.
- Use poignant pictures.
- Select meaningful colors.
- Integrate with your verbal identity.

Learn more about logos, colors, and design for nonprofits in future chapters of this book.

Verbalize

Every nonprofit has an important story to tell. The key is communicating it so people listen and take action. It's expressing visually and verbally what a nonprofit does, what makes it unique and why stakeholders should support the mission.

Putting into words the essence of a nonprofit brand is paramount to success. A cogent message platform articulates the soul of a brand and must blend with a visually compelling story to create a single voice. Today, we are overwhelmed with information and to "strike a responsive chord" requires crafting a verbal identity that penetrates the mind and reaches into the subconscious where words hold meaning.

The message platform or verbal identity includes several essential elements that must be communicated across all channels, including:

- Name and tagline.
- About us.
- Vision and mission statements.
- Key messages.
- Audience-specific messages.

Composing a verbal identity is a little like writing lyrics to a song, but instead you are writing a collection of messages that form a single communications platform. Like melody and music, messages should sing and entertain us! Words can work independently or in harmony with each other and visual communication to inform, influence, and inspire audiences across multiple mediums and channels.

Consistent, credible messages delivered to the right audience, in the right medium, and at the right time and place work best. Know your audience. What makes them tick? Strive for clarity and use as few words as possible. Seek words and messages that resonate emotionally with your target audience.

The verbal identity should be extended to a nonprofit's full line of communications materials and products, including websites, newsletters, fact sheets, annual reports, press releases, and fundraising tools. Test messages for their ability to grab audiences and utilize different media to touch all brand points of contact.

Read more about verbal branding, naming, taglines, message development, and articulating your vision and mission in later chapters of this book.

Promote

Nonprofits, like businesses, must proactively and consistently promote their brand, products, and services, especially their benefits and value to society. Your organization won't sustain and grow by "doing good" alone. Getting your name out in the community will help to fill the treasury for noble causes and build a reliable fan base. Promote your brand to also win hearts and minds and to start and continue conversations that will yield lasting relationships and loyal supporters.

Brand promotion begins by putting the target audience at the center of all outreach activities and extends to everything your organization does, from answering the phone to the way services are delivered. It's creating a positive emotional experience with your brand at every point of contact.

So how do you get the word out and build brand buzz? Know your audiences, their needs and wants and align them with your brand strategy, goal, objectives, and mission. Gain a marketing edge by connecting with stakeholders where they live, work, and play, whether it's at a neighborhood event, in school, at the mall, or on the job.

Leverage Your Brand Champions

The best brand advocates are those who live their organization's vision and purpose every day. Your staff, volunteers, the board of directors, and partners who already believe in your cause act as brand champions for spreading the message and building name recognition.

Brand champions are on the front lines every day and can help your nonprofit build relationships with stakeholders through dialogue, speaking engagements, and face-to-face encounters. Make sure the team has current message points so everyone speaks in one voice. Testimonials from service recipients, too, can help your nonprofit become word on the street.

Identify brand touch points, (places where, when, and how stakeholders come in contact with your organization's visual and verbal identities) and communication channels that present the best opportunities to reach the target audience.

Use an Integrated Marketing Approach

Take an integrated marketing approach that utilizes a full marketing mix, including print and online media, earned media (news releases), direct mail, Internet marketing, special events, promotions, and social media to achieve the best outcomes. Use your marketing budget wisely based on target audience analysis. Consider how stakeholders come in contact with your organization and how they are most likely to receive messages about it.

Below are just a few of many marketing tools and communications venues that your nonprofit can use to promote its brand, including:

- Website and social media.
- Annual reports, brochures, and fact sheets.
- Press releases and success stories.
- Public service announcements.
- Posters, post cards, and promotional items.
- Special events (conferences and open houses).

Working with Celebrity Spokespersons

Celebrities can raise visibility and add credibility to your message by doing public service announcements (PSAs) and making special appearances. You'll need to carefully select a celebrity who supports your mission and is willing to work for your cause.

High-profile spokespersons come with many benefits, but also pose risks and potential drawbacks should a negative event or circumstance occur. Working with celebrities can be challenging due to scheduling conflicts and unclear expectations. Do your homework.

If you find the right fit, working with a celebrity spokesperson can build brand recognition fast. Learn more about celebrities and their causes at looktothestars.org, and consider high-profile spokespersons with ties to your community. *A check this out*

Making Smart Decisions

Clearly, nonprofits have an array of options to promote their brand, yet limited funding and resources to get the job done. Whether you seek star power in a celebrity or the quiet effectiveness of an e-newsletter, you'll need to make smart marketing decisions based on your budget, audience, and primary objectives.

Protect

Think of your nonprofit's brand as a sacred treasure that must be shielded from pillage or plunder, intentional or not. Your logo, tagline, and intellectual property are valued assets and it would be wise to keep their integrity intact. You can protect your brand from infringement by taking three basic steps that will require some time but not significant resources.

1) Obtain trademarks for logos and taglines to prevent misuse or confusion in the marketplace. A trademark is any unique word, symbol, logo, or name used to distinguish the goods and services of a company or organization. Work with the United States Patent and Trademarks Office to officially register a trademark. The process usually takes several months or more, but is well worth it. Similarly, go through the United States Copyright Office to record documents, such as books, songs, and other creative works.

2.) Develop a Graphic Standards Manual and Editorial Style Guide to create consistency across your visual and verbal identities. Establishing graphic standards protects your brand by ensuring everyone follows a uniform approach to creating visual impressions. Without guidelines, your brand may become fragmented and diluted with a motley gallery of many different logos, colors, and typefaces.

The purpose of the Graphic Standards Manual is to get everyone working on the same page. In branding, the sum is greater than the parts. Make sure your manual includes proper usage guidelines and "do's and don'ts" for your logo, tagline, and colors used across multiple communications channels and mediums. Over time, a consistent brand identity will stick in the minds of stakeholders and strengthen affiliation with your nonprofit.

An Editorial Style Guide is a valuable tool that succinctly outlines your nonprofit's language style and usage in print and electronic media. It helps writers, editors, and other nonprofit communicators to convey information in a single voice and consistent format. An Editorial Style Guide must be unique to your organization and should be revised regularly to stay fresh and relevant to your current communications environment.

Commonly used guides include *The Associated Press Stylebook*, *The Chicago Manual of Style*, and the *Publication Manual of the American Psychological Association* or APA Style. Federal agencies use the *U.S. Government Printing Office (GPO) Style Manual*. Many Editorial Style Guides used by nonprofits include sections on capitalization, numbers, naming conventions, grammar, acronyms, abbreviations, and language that describes the organization and its purpose.

Your Graphic Standards Manual and Editorial Style Guide may be more than 100 pages each with lots of samples or just a one-page tip sheet that helps remind everyone to follow the visual and verbal identity usage guidelines.

3) Entrust designated communications staff to monitor proper usage of both established graphic standards and editorial style guidelines. Someone should ensure that the guides are updated as needed and distributed to new staff or outside consultants who write for the organization. Training should be provided to staff so they understand the established guidelines.

Refine

Brands grow, mature, and need constant refinement to stay current in an evolving marketplace. Without change, brands become stale, boring, and lose their muscle. Micro-adjustments and sometimes major facelifts are necessary to prevent visual and verbal identities from becoming outdated.

Names, logos, and visual identities are often updated to mirror a modern, forward thinking image. Nonprofits change their names, but not without costs and serious evaluation. Changing a name requires revising the articles of incorporation, along with all communications materials, and implementing a marketing plan to get the word out.

Messages, too, are refined to reflect a new strategic direction and brand meaning. Change should occur only after careful analysis reveals something simply isn't working. Each brand element works independently, yet is part of a total marketing package. So while the messaging may need refining the logo may not. The other R pillar of nonprofit branding, "Research," should form the basis of all brand refinement decisions.

Change is good but should be prompted by internal and external factors and backed by sound audience research. Know why you are making brand adjustments and what the impact will be on your nonprofit's image, bottom line, and meaning to stakeholders.

When Change is Good

Factors that often drive brand refinement include:
1) Confusion in the marketplace or a lack of clarity.
2) A merger with another nonprofit that necessitates a change to reflect the new brand.
3) A major change in the mission or purpose of the organization.
4) Narrowing the focus of the organization to a specific cause.

5) A name that no longer reflects current nomenclature or a visual identity that needs refreshing after many years of service.

In 2010, for the first time in 43 years, the YMCA unveiled a new brand strategy to increase understanding of the impact the nonprofit makes in communities. The new brand strategy was the result of two years of analysis and research, according to the YMCA. A new, more forward-thinking logo now reflects the vibrancy and diversity of the organization, and a framework that centers on three core areas: youth development, healthy living, and social responsibility. In another major change, the nonprofit has adopted "the Y" as its brand name to align with how people most commonly refer to the organization, although it will continue to use YMCA as its formal name.

The Y's former logo was last updated in 1967, and was the organization's sixth since its inception more than 160 years ago. The goal of the refreshed logo, with its multiple color options and new contemporary look, is to better depict the vibrancy of the Y and the diversity of the communities it serves. The new logo's bold, active, and welcoming shape symbolizes the YMCA's commitment to personal and social progress.

Of course, change is not always welcome by everyone. The Village People, which recorded the 1978 hit song "Y.M.C.A." that's still played at ballgames today, publically expressed disappointment with the new name. Over time, audiences usually warm-up to changes in brands but it can take some getting use to and a proactive marketing plan. The key is doing your homework and ensuring that change will achieve a desired outcome or objective.

Chapter 5

Winning the Name Game

Intense love does not measure, it just gives.
– Mother Teresa

What do Xerox, Google, Nike, Habitat for Humanity, and Make-A-Wish Foundation have in common? They are all successful companies and nonprofit organizations that played the name game and won.

Naming your organization is one of the most important business decisions you will ever make. About 75 percent of all consumer purchases are made because of a company name or brand. It's what Scott Bedbury, the marketing guru behind Starbucks and Nike, termed "brand belonging." Of course, a good name can't save a bad company or nonprofit. But a good name will differentiate you from competitors, connect with customers, and build your brand over time.

So how did some of the top nonprofits and companies create their magical names? The Salvation Army, according to the nonprofit's history, was originally called the Christian Mission. William Booth, who co-founded the nonprofit along side his wife, Catherine, was reading a printer's proof of the 1878 Annual Report when he the noticed the statement, "The Christian Mission under the Superintendent's of the Rev. William Booth is a volunteer army." He crossed out the words "Volunteer Army'" and penned in "Salvation Army."

In 1937, a new way of copying called Xerography was invented by law student Chester Carlson. The name Xerox was then created and later trademarked. Like Monster.com, Yahoo was once thought of as an off-the-wall name, but it stuck.

Created in 1971, Nike means the "Greek Goddess of Victory." The Nike name, swoosh, and tagline, Just Do It., became marketing history. Also created in 1971, Starbucks Coffee opened its doors in Seattle and was named after the first mate in Herman Melville's Moby Dick. There are lots of brown cows, says marketing expert Seth Godin, but a purple cow is truly remarkable. Take a risk, but don't be absurd.

Coming up with the right name can be challenging. Not only do you have to find a name that garners attention and is easy to say, but it also has to be available. Check the Trademark Office website (www.uspto.gov) and do a search for names in your industry. Also, visit Register.com to see which domain names have been taken. You really don't need to do focus groups to discover the right name, but you should test it on your employees and stakeholders. Make sure your name is not offensive to people in another language. Below are some basic guidelines and rules that naming experts often use to create names.

Make it easy to say

Remember, the average person is bombarded with thousands of messages a day. So make sure that your name is short, simple, and reduces confusion. Your organization's name can even be fun to say. It should find its way into the hearts and minds of your stakeholders and employees.

Make it stand out

Try to create a unique name. With a little creativity, you can develop a name that is truly memorable. Dare to be different. Give your name a personality.

Link your name to your mission

When brainstorming for a name, it's a good ideal, when possible, to link your name to your mission and values. Your name should mirror the nature of your nonprofit and its unique purpose in the community.

Avoid acronyms

Many leading naming and marketing experts generally do not like to use initials or acronyms in corporate naming. Sure, they have worked for many companies, such as America Online (AOL), but the result is a meaningless stream of letters that often leave people confused and uninspired. Many nonprofit organizations and associations become known by their acronyms, but only after time and significant marketing investment. Focus on ensuring your name tells your story rather than a catchy acronym.

Consider made-up names

A hot trend in company or product naming is transparent or contrived names. These names often have no initial dictionary meaning and stretch the English language, but they can be effective. It has worked for Facebook, Verizon, Cingular and Accenture. Made-up names can take on the image the company creates, but it may be at the cost of considerable marketing and advertising. Nonprofits need to think carefully about this approach to naming.

Use Alliteration

Nonprofit or corporate naming really is all about linguistics. Use alliteration, crisp consonants, and vowels to tell your story. The mind remembers names that use this technique. Some examples are Habitat for Humanity International, Catholic Charities, Dirt Devil, Rolls Royce, Intel Inside, Blackberry, Dunkin' Donuts, Krispy Kreme, and Coca-Cola.

So what's in a name? Everything the mind can imagine. Justice Oliver Wendell Holmes said, "A man's mind, once stretched, never goes back to its original dimensions." Create a memorable name that inspires us. That's how the name game is won.

Say it with a Tagline

Catchy jingles, slogans, and taglines. Call them what you will. They extend a brand's meaning and personality beyond the name alone. Nike and "Just do it." Avis and "We try harder." And Energizer's renowned bunny and "Keep Going."

These remarkable brand names and taglines form powerful combinations that have been burned into our consciousness for decades. Think of your nonprofit's name and tagline as a dynamic marketing duo that can increase brand recognition and reach.

And while some of the most popular phrases have come from the commercial side, many taglines crafted by or for nonprofits, too, have made their mark. For example, the United Way's LIVE UNITED, the Salvation Army's "DOING THE MOST GOOD," and the California Milk Processor Board's "Got Milk?" campaigns all inspire us. In 2011, the United Negro College Fund (UNCF) celebrated the 40th anniversary of its famous motto, "The mind is a terrible thing to waste."

Great taglines entertain us. They instantly connect with us in a special way, stirring our emotions and making us think and act. They stick to us like glue and give added relevance to brands. For nonprofit communicators, creating a successful tagline is challenging, but when done correctly can be among the most rewarding things you can do.

Tagline Essentials

So how do you create an effective tagline that resonates with target audiences? Here are some tips that I have learned creating taglines for nonprofits, government agencies, and corporations.

- Make it memorable and persuasive.
- Originality counts.
- Keep it simple (five words or less).
- Action verbs work (save, build, discover).
- Conjure up a picture in the mind.
- Say what your nonprofit's name alone can't.

In addition, here are several pitfalls to avoid when writing your tagline.

- Don't do taglines by committee.
- Avoid using "the best and only."
- Never forget your audience.

Test Your Tagline

Taglines should be tested with stakeholders before going to market to ensure their best chance for success. Develop two or three prototypes to share with participants in a focus group or interviews to get reaction. Since taglines appear next to the logo but also unaccompanied in written context, I first like to create text only versions to get feedback not influenced by graphic design treatment. Then present design concepts to illustrate how the tagline appears alone and in combination with the name. You know that you have an effective tagline if it's well received both in the text and design forms.

Ask the group questions about the likeability, clarity, understanding, and meaning of the tagline and whether it effectively communicates the essence of your brand. Collect audience insights to make a final decision and refine the tagline, if necessary. Balance what the audience tells you about the tagline with what you know about your brand and effective messaging. The end result will be a tagline that reflects valid perceptions and professional development.

Nonprofits that do not yet have a tagline should strongly consider creating one. A tagline will enrich your brand, adding personality and feeling to your good name. But guard against changing your tagline often. Only change your tagline when it no longer has brand relevance or appeal. It can take considerable marketing and time for taglines to build a level of recognition with target audiences.

Birth of a Brand: Excel Beyond the Bell

Creating a brand is a little like giving birth. Like babies, brands must first undergo a development phase before their beauty is ready for the world to behold. Brands, too, need nurturing, protection, love, and acceptance. Brands also mature, develop personalities all their own, and get stronger by building emotional connections to people.

Montgomery County, Maryland is home to nearly 1 million increasingly economically and culturally diverse people and the demand for quality out-of-school time programs for children and youth is extremely high. The Montgomery County Collaboration Council for Children, Youth and Families, Inc. worked closely with Image One PR to create a brand designed to build excitement about the county's out-of-school time system, while striking a responsive chord with stakeholders.

During the initial Discovery Phase, much was learned about what stakeholders were saying about after school youth development in Montgomery County. Significant input was sought from key stakeholders about the branding process. In all, more than 130 stakeholders participated in the branding process, including Montgomery County Collaboration Council staff and board members, children, youth, parents, funders, afterschool/youth development providers, businesses, and representatives from the county schools, county employees, police, and the Commission on Children and Youth.

A Brand Strategy was created that included information about naming, vision and mission statements, core identity, brand personality, target audiences, logo, tagline, color selection, and brand traits.

After testing several concepts, Excel Beyond the Bell was born. The logo is highly functional and presents a powerful image of fun, energy, youth engagement, warmth, pursuit of excellence, professionalism, and achievement. The letters are bold, modern, and easy to read. The blue and purple logo colors were overwhelmingly favored by stakeholders. Blue signifies harmony, cool, understanding, and tranquility. Purple is a popular choice among children and youth and conveys creativity, energy, and passion.

Excel Beyond the Bell reflects Montgomery County Public School's (MCPS) reputation for excellence. The school system earned a 2010 Malcolm Baldrige National Quality Award, the highest honor given to American organizations for performance excellence. MCPS became only the sixth public school system to receive the award and is the largest school district to be a recipient.

Excel Beyond the Bell was accompanied by a tagline, *Laugh, Learn, Achieve*. The tagline evokes fun, academic enrichment, inspiration, accomplishment, and a commitment to doing your best. The tagline is short, simple, and easy to remember.

"We wanted to create an inspiring, fun brand that strikes a responsive chord with out-of-school time audiences," said Carol Walsh, Executive Director, Montgomery County Collaboration Council for Children, Youth and Families, Inc. "Excel Beyond the Bell connects not only with potential partners and funders, but also with children, youth, and parents. Important to the naming process is getting input from key stakeholders so everyone feels they are part of the process."

The Vision: All Montgomery County children and youth will be successful in school and in life. We see children and youth making smart choices, improving academic performance, discovering their talents, strengthening life skills, and preparing themselves for adulthood.

The Mission: To inspire children and youth to realize their full potential by building a sustainable system offering safe, quality, and accessible out-of-school time programs.

Brand Attributes and Personality Traits

The following brand attributes support the core identity:

EXCELLENCE
Expressed by: Creating high standards and a professional development system, attention to quality, performance management, continuous improvement, monitoring, committed, and credentials/quality of staff.

INCLUSIVE
Expressed by: Accessibility, affordability, diversity, unified, connected, teamwork, and all together.

INSPIRING
Expressed by: Enthusiasm, high energy, vibrant, engaging programs, motivating, generating excitement, and uplifting.

ENRICHING
Expressed by: Educational, uplifting, fulfilling, achievement, enlightening, artistic, creative, rewarding, constructive, and helpful.

CARING
Expressed by: Compassion, empathy, respect, giving, generous, love of life, humanity, sympathy, comfort, patience, understanding, and kindness.

As stakeholders become more familiar with the Excel Beyond the Bell brand, the following personality traits become more evident.

FUN
Expressed by: Laughter, joy, humor, smiles, cheer, good times, enjoyment, play, relaxation, and entertainment.

FRIENDLY
Expressed by: Friendship, helpful, teamwork, sharing, receptive, affable, attentive, welcoming, open, sociable, and genial.

ENERGETC
Expressed by: High energy, engagement, lively, vital, vibrant, sprightly, fresh, enterprising, eager, and bright.

Award-Winning Brand

The branding process also involved creation of messaging, a website, brochure, e-newsletter and a video, "Time to Excel." The Excel Beyond the Bell branding elements and supporting communications products earned national recognition, receiving APEX, Ava, Hermes Creative, MarCom, Silver Communicator, and Telly Awards.

Chapter 6

Great Design for Good Causes

I saw the angel in the marble and carved until I set him free.
– Michelangelo

Today, in our highly visual world, graphic design has a powerful impact on driving positive social change. Great design has the remarkable ability to inform, motivate, entertain, and inspire us to take action. Vibrant posters that convince us to give generously or daring bumper stickers that influence our behavior are products of effective design.

Excellence in design occurs when we can clearly communicate our message using aesthetics to achieve a specific outcome or objective. It's putting both the creative and rational sides of the brain to work to master the art and science of persuasion.

In college, while working for a bookstore, I became fascinated by a 1979 New York Times best-selling book, *"Drawing on the Right Side of the Brain,"* by Dr. Betty Edward. The groundbreaking book, which has twice been revised, sheds light on how the brain affects drawing. Both sides of the brain are involved in most human activities. However, the left hemisphere of the brain primarily controls verbal, logical, and analytical thinking, while the right hemisphere is dominant for creativity, visual imagery, music, emotions, and spatial abilities. The left half and right half don't always know what the other half is doing. This disconnect causes what design expert Marty Neumeier calls "the brand gap."

The challenge for nonprofit communicators is bridging the divide and bringing out the best strategy and creativity. The result will be compelling ideas and striking design that originates from the full richness of the mind. One brain, two cerebral hemispheres, 100 billion neurons, and infinite doors to grand design and a better world.

What makes compelling graphic design? It depends on who you talk to and what you are trying to achieve. Supreme Court Justice Potter Stewart once observed that he could not define obscenity, "but I know it when I see it." We all form opinions about design based on our own unique perceptions, culture, and experiences. Through our senses, especially our eyes, we absorb information that gets quickly tagged as meaningful or irrelevant. The more the five senses are involved, the stronger the response. So when we encounter an aesthetically pleasing design it immediately evokes emotion.

> **One brain, two cerebral hemispheres, 100 billion neurons, and infinite doors to grand design and a better world.**

The Dual Forces of Design

Graphic design is really about aesthetics – the study of beauty. The term aesthetics comes to us from the ancient Greeks whose philosophy on splendor and perception had the greatest influence on Western culture. Vibrant visual communication embodies ideas, intelligence, intensity, and emotional energy. It blends classical elements of design, including shapes, lines, color, type, text, art, illustration, symbols, and photography to create visual appeal.

In his 1872 book, "*The Birth of Tragedy*," German Philosopher Friedrich Nietzsche theorized that great art resulted from a fusion of

Dionysian and Apollonian forces. In Greek mythology, Apollo and Dionysus are gods of the creative arts but hold completely opposite personalities. Apollo is associated with reason, structure, and order, while Dionysus mirrors chaos, freedom, and emotion. The "artistic impulses" of both personalities yield the finest art forms. Didn't many famous classic and contemporary creative artists possess these very dual traits, including Michelangelo, Pablo Picasso, Vincent Van Gogh, Georgia O' Keeffe, Andy Warhol, Ludwig van Beethoven, Jim Morrison, Ray Charles, and Edgar Allan Poe?

In modern terms, great design truly combines multiple principles and elements depending on its intent, including reason, chaos, symmetry, balance, simplicity, complexity, harmony, light, darkness, perfection, and expression. Salient design speaks to us, often reflecting tradition, history, culture, humanity, nature, thought, and the future.

Push the Creative Envelope

Nonprofits interested in taking their visual communication to the next level should push the creative envelope and become rebels with a cause. Try new ideas and concepts that differentiate your organization, its mission, and marketing campaigns. Be visionary.

We often hear "think outside the box," but who put us in a box in the first place? In other words, create freely and without borders. Never, however, lose sight of your design purpose and audience. Think and feel as your audience does and the inspiration will come. Test your designs to determine their value to intended stakeholders.

Let Images Tell Your Story

Use compelling images to evoke emotions. The best photographs and images are those actually generated by your organization, but be selective. Quality is key. If needed, turn to stock photography to get the image you need. I often use Shutterstock, iStockphoto, Getty

Images, Veer, Corbis, and Punchstock. All of these services provide excellent search engines for finding what you need. Use royalty free images to avoid time and usage restrictions.

Simple, Yet Powerful Symbols Work

 I have always been energized by two of the world's most recognized icons – the ubiquitous peace symbol and Smiley face. These simple, yet powerful icons inspire good. They are perfect examples of how design can have a positive impact on society and work that matters.

The peace symbol turned 50 in 2008 and was first introduced to promote nuclear disarmament. It continues today as a popular and powerful icon for social change in America. The symbol is everywhere and has regained popularity as a fashion icon for clothing and merchandise. Likewise, the famous Smiley face still brightens our day with a sunny outlook and good cheer. Artist Harvey Ball invented Smiley in 1963 for use on buttons. Little did he know that the happy face would become a beloved sign for joy. Each generation seeks new symbols, pop icons, and meaning, but the Peace symbol and Smiley face have endured and remain relevant today.

Making it Happen

Creating the right idea at the right time can have dramatic impact. The possibilities are endless, but you have to lay a solid foundation for success. Great design does not happen by accident. Below are some pointers learned from personal experience working with dozens of award-winning designers over two decades.

- Hire professional graphic designers with degrees, specialties, and training in their respective field, usually the fine arts. Look for demonstrated success in print and online design.

Check their portfolio for creative flair and range across diverse assignments.

- Start design projects with a Creative Brief that outlines the goal, objectives, target audience, timeline, messages, and purpose.
- Create a collaborative process that nurtures creativity and balances great design with sound strategy.
- Don't dilute quality and stifle creativity by letting strategists dictate design. Strike a balance and avoid "design by committee." Stand by established design principles and elements to keep design integrity intact.

Graphic design turns the ordinary into the extraordinary. Invest in developing creative works that help your nonprofit to connect with stakeholders. Don't skimp on the quality of visual communications, despite critics who claim that nonprofit marketing should not be overly done. Efficient and effective design are never wasteful. We only remember what is memorable.

Putting "Swoosh" in Your Logo

Striking logos flirt with us. They arouse the senses and catch our eye. We are smitten by their beauty, charm, and personality. It's love at first sight and we hope it leads to a meaningful relationship that lasts a lifetime. Every logo tells a story and has a critical purpose: to create a distinctive mark that separates an organization from the competition. If "a picture is worth a thousand words," then the value of a logo is much more.

The best nonprofit logos are priceless. Far beyond their ability to raise revenues, they build a special bond with stakeholders who believe in what an organization stands for and in its purpose. A logo, which is short for logotypes and in Greek means *word*, is a key piece of your brand puzzle. But it is only as good as the character behind it. Great logos and quality brands work together.

The good news for nonprofits is that logo development and refinement should not break your budget. Did you know that Nike's Swoosh trademark was literally done on a shoestring budget? The Nike "Swoosh" is simple, fluid, fast, and was very affordable.

In 1971, according to Nike's corporate history, company founder Bill Knight was supplementing his modest income from his fledgling Blue Ribbon Sport Inc. by teaching at Portland State University. He met Carolyn Davidson, a graphic design student, who created the now famous brand icon for just $35.00. American Record Breaker Steve Prefontaine then became the first major track athlete to wear the Nike brand shoes. And in 1988, the "Just do it." tagline was chosen by Ad Age as one of the top two taglines of the 20th Century. The campaign is now ensconced in the Smithsonian National Museum.

Like the Nike "Swoosh," some of the best logo designs of nonprofits are simple and forward thinking and they resonate instantly. Think of the American Red Cross, Goodwill Industries International, and the new YMCA logo, "the Y." Modern logo design requires expressing an idea with compelling images, colors, typeface, and illustrations that exert graphic power and emotional appeal. Simplicity and directness allow the viewer to connect instantly.

Whether you are refining a logo or creating a new one, there are some standards and guidelines that can help you succeed. Successful logos connect with viewers by building trust, evoking emotion, and establishing credibility. Effective logos build upon several design elements.

Forward Thinking

Does your logo project the future and does it reflect the latest design trends, curves, lines, typefaces, shapes, and colors? Your logo should mirror your mission and keep your organization on the cutting edge.

Defined and Distinctive

A logo should define your organization. It must be unique and not be confused with other logos in the nonprofit sector. It should standout but not be unappealing or hard to understand. It should portray the essence of your nonprofit.

Functionality and Format

Keep in mind how your logo will be used. It must be visually effective in multiple media forms and environments, including on signs, packaging, letterhead, faxes, brochures, and online. It must work well in a variety of sizes.

Three Basic Logo Types

Nearly all logos can be organized into three basic types: 1) Logotypes or words only 2) Abstract symbols or icons only or 3) Combination words and a symbol. Text only logos are very popular and generally are easier to develop. Examples include the Muscular Dystrophy Association (MDA), Xerox, IBM, and Sony. These logos use type treatments with a little twist to make them distinctive.

Abstract logos contain icons and images that depict what a company or organization does, such as when a nonprofit uses a heart or hands to convey its mission. Corporate examples include

Shell Oil, Apple, and Nike with the "Swoosh." The World Wildlife Fund's (WWF) panda bear, the 4-H clovers, and the Red Cross are well-known symbols among nonprofits.

Because abstract logos have no inherent meaning, it often takes a long time and lots of marketing and advertising to get them established in the marketplace. The nonprofit trend today is using combined text and a symbol to achieve a single effect. Examples of nonprofits that blend a word mark with an iconic image include the Salvation Army, Habitat for Humanity, and the American Cancer Society.

Whether your nonprofit is new or established, a logo is critical to communicating with target audiences. Put some swoosh and style in your logo and let it help your organization go places.

The Psychology of Colors

Colors make the brand. Coke is red. Pepsi is blue. Choosing the right dominate and complementary colors for your nonprofit is critical to success. Every quality brand must live up to its promise, but there's no mistaking the power of colors in building strong and loyal brand connections.

But what do colors mean? The emotions and moods evoked by colors depend on past experiences, nationality, and personal preferences. However, studies indicate that specific colors and their combinations have a psychological effect on the majority of people. Here are several popular colors, their meaning, and common uses today.

The Passion of Red

Red is the most emotionally intense color and it's known to stimulate a faster heartbeat and breathing. Of course, it's also the color of blood, passion, and love. Red conveys energy, action, and power, but it can appear confrontational and intimidating. Red cars are very popular targets for thieves. Because of its visibility, red is used for stop signs, lights, and fire trucks. Apples, tomatoes, and cherries are red.

Red is an attention getter and is often used by decorators as an accent. Restaurants often use red as a decorating color to stimulate appetite. Entirely red rooms, however, can make people anxious. Remember "The Shining" by Stephen King? Red is the color used by some of the world's most renowned organizations, companies, and brands, including the American Red Cross, the Salvation Army, Coca-Cola, Toyota, and the Chicago Bulls. In China, red implies good luck and is used for weddings. In Russia, red means beautiful. Roses are red.

The Power of Yellow

Yellow is a primary color that is very powerful and can be eye-fatiguing. It has many shades. It speeds metabolism and causes eye irritation, but it also makes a great highlighter if used sparingly. Yellow rooms make babies cry. People lose their tempers more often in yellow rooms. Lemons, school buses, and the sun are yellow. Yellow means proceed with caution.

Yellow is a color used effectively by LIVESTRONG, McDonald's, and Shell Oil. In Burma and Egypt, yellow is a color of mourning.

The Attraction of Orange

Orange is another color that attracts attention. It's associated with warmth, cheerfulness, and friendliness. Like red, orange is an excellent appetite stimulant. It's also popular at Halloween. Pumpkins and carrots are orange. Think Home Depot, MasterCard, and the Baltimore Orioles.

The Popularity of Blue

Blue is the most popular color and is easy on the eyes. Blue signifies tranquility, harmony, patience, and understanding. Its potential negative qualities are passiveness, coldness, and depression. Blue is also a natural appetite suppressant and is generally not a good choice for restaurant decor. Blue relaxes people.

Wearing blue to an interview indicates loyalty. Studies show that students and weight lifters perform better in blue rooms. The sky and the ocean are blue. It's the color used by many nonprofits and corporations, including the Boys and Girls Club of America, JetBlue, Exxon, Ford, and Blue Cross Blue Shield.

The Freshness of Green

Green has many symbiotic meanings. The most common is nature. Green in the United States is the color of money. Green signifies good health, life, youth, freshness, and vigor. Green means go.

However, green can also reflect envy and greed. Green is the easiest color on the eyes and can help improve vision. Like blue, green has a calming effect on the nervous system. It's a popular color in hospitals and waiting rooms because it relaxes people. Think Girl Scouts of the USA, 4-H, John Deere, Starbucks, and the Green Bay Packers. Green is the national color of Ireland.

The Style of Black

Black is a color of authority. It speaks with power, style, mystery, elegance, and sophistication. It may also symbolize evil, death, and mourning. Priests wear black because it signifies submission to God. Black is popular in fashion because it makes people look thinner.

The Reliability of Brown

Brown is solid and reliable. It's the color of earth and wood. It creates an open and neutral environment. It projects credibility, strength, and maturity. Brown is the corporate color for United Parcel Service (UPS). "What Can Brown Do for You?" Men favor brown.

The Creativity of Purple

Purple is the color for royalties and often represents wealth, nobility, and passion. Purple is artistic, feminine, and romantic. Purple stimulates creativity. Cleopatra, the Egyptian queen, loved purple. It's the team color for the Minnesota Vikings. And don't forget Prince in the Purple Rain.

The Many Uses of White

White reflects light and is an excellent base color. Brides wear white. So do doctors and nurses to imply sterility. White symbolizes innocence and purity. But it also shows dirt and is harder to keep clean. A white dove conveys peace and a white flag is the universal symbol for truce. White means morning in China and Japan.

PART III

Nonprofit Communications: Let's Talk

Chapter 7

The Language of Nonprofits

Words can sometimes, in moments of grace, attain the quality of deeds.
Elie Wiesel

Go to a baseball game and you'll hear familiar chatter echo throughout the stadium. "Programs Here. Popcorn. Hot Dogs. Cotton Candy." They will play tunes like "Take me out to the ball game" or the Village People's famous Y.M.C.A. song. This is the language and music of baseball.

Nonprofits, too, have a language all their own. Sure, there are many nonprofits and each communicates in its own unique way. But there is a common voice among nonprofits. It's a language filled with lots of four-letter words, such as love, hope, give, heal, and care. These poignant words and many others universally appeal to our emotions. Nonprofit language attempts to inspire us to take action for a worthy cause.

> give **inspire** hope *love* help **lead** move
> **save** protect *nurture* support trust **feed**
> educate **peace** joy **care** guide nourish bridge
> build **strengthen** develop create energize *unite*
> *thank* **volunteer** raise **dream** overcome
> connect succeed **improve** *heart* unite

Nonprofits that master the art of writing and communicating their vision, mission, and message will put their organization on solid footing and a swifter path to success.

Practice Plain Language Writing

So what are the qualities of rigorous nonprofit writing? And how do you craft language with bite and edge? Writing is complex. It's a painstaking process that takes lots of hard work. Nonprofit writers, too, have the tough job of moving hearts and minds.

You can improve your ability to communicate by sharpening your plain language writing skills. Here are several points of emphasis I have learned through more than 30,000 hours of writing since college.

1. **Think like your audience.** Who are you writing to and for what purpose? Are you speaking to volunteers, service recipients, funders, or potential partners? Strike a responsive chord by putting yourself in the reader's shoes.

2. **Write clearly.** Make sure readers can understand what you are trying to say. Strive for clarity and readability. Get to your point quickly. Eliminate "gobbledygook" and jargon.

3. **Be concise.** Precision counts. Choose your words wisely. Each word should have a distinct purpose. The less complex your writing, the clearer and stronger your message. Keep it tight and forceful.

4. **Use active voice.** Avoid using "was, is, are, and were" as the main verb of the sentence. In active voice, the subject of the sentence performs the work. (Active) The dog bit the man. (Passive) The man was bitten by the dog.

5. **Apply balance and rhythm.** Good writing facilitates easy reading. It moves us along with a steady pace like the beat

of a song. Mix longer sentences with shorter ones. Ensure the copy flows and is logical. Watch your transitions.

6. **Edit and proofread your work.** Go back to your writing. Refine it. Tighten the language. Read it over for clarity and understanding. If possible, let another set of trained eyes review and copyedit your work for errors.

10 Tips for the Everyday Writer

Below are several language tips you might find useful in your daily writing. Many writers commonly miss these little gems.

- Tip 1: Say the *public* and not the *general public* - the public is already general.
- Tip 2: Avoid writing *in order to*. Write *to respond* instead of *in order to respond*.
- Tip 3: Avoid overuse of *as well as*. Use *and* instead.
- Tip 4: *Farther* relates to distance and *further* denotes advancement to a greater degree. Read *further*. Go *farther* down stream.
- Tip 5: *Between* is used with two people or things. *Among* is used with three or more people or things.
- Tip 6: Do not abbreviate decades. Write the *1960s*, not the *1960's*.
- Tip 7: Do not use *that* when noting people. He is the first writer *who* ever missed the contest. Nonprofits *that* start fundraising early raise more money.
- Tip 8: *Accept* is to receive or take and *except* is to exclude. I run everyday *except* Friday. I *accept* your invitation to speak.
- Tip 9: Use *between you and me* and not *between you and I*.
- Tip 10: *It's* is a contraction for "it is." *It's* raining outside. *Its* is the possessive form of it. The snake shed its skin.

Beyond the Fundamentals

Mastering the writing fundamentals will help you to craft clear and convincing copy. It may even remove warts and wrinkles from your writing. But taking writing to a higher level relies on rich imagination and creativity that comes from our inner mind. Here we get persuasive prose for polished marketing messages and materials.

Writers draw heavily upon their life experiences, what they have learned from other writers who influence their style and thinking, and available resources on language and writing. We all have our favorites. I love Stephen King because he tells great stories. Ernest Hemmingway wrote with strength and remarkable clarity. Walt Whitman composed beautiful poetry with purpose and powerful imagery. The beloved works of Shel Silverstein, Amy Tan, and Maya Angelou, too, paint vivid pictures.

Several excellent books on language and writing include *The Elements of Style* by William Strunk Jr. and E.B. White; *The Deluxe Transitive Vampire: The Ultimate Handbook of Grammar for the Innocent, the Eager, and the Doomed* by Karen Elizabeth Gordon; and *Grammar Girl's Quick and Dirty Tips for Better Writing* by Mignon Fogarty.

Writing Vision and Mission Statements

Most vision and mission statements are not memorized word for word, but instead are recalled by their core meaning. Effective statements capture the spirit and essence of your organization very quickly.

A vision statement is that special place "over the rainbow where skies are blue." It's realizing the big dream. It's seeing the future and accomplishing ultimate outcomes. It paints an instant picture filled with promise. Not all nonprofits have vision statements, but really should as an extension of their verbal identity.

Mission statements focus on an organization's primary goal and the process for achieving it. They serve as the guiding light that nonprofits live by daily. Both vision and mission statements must be clear and concise. Try to keep each statement under 20 words. The problem begins when nonprofits add too much detail. Focus on the single thing your nonprofit does best.

Don't make the mistake of integrating your vision and mission statements with your organization's history and description. Vision and mission statements should stand alone so they stand out. Seek input from your board, staff, and volunteers to determine what words best describe your nonprofit's vision and mission.

Below are examples of effective nonprofit vision and mission statements.

Vision Statements

Save the Children

A world in which every child attains the right to survival, protection, development and participation.

Ducks Unlimited

Wetlands sufficient to fill the skies with waterfowl today, tomorrow and forever.

Mission Statements

Michael & Susan Dell Foundation

Transforming lives of children living in urban poverty through better health and education.

American Heart Association

Building healthier lives, free of cardiovascular diseases and stroke.

Place your vision and mission statements where people can see them – on your website, in office spaces, in publications, and wherever your organization communicates what it does and why.

Creating Core Values

Not all nonprofits state their core values, but those that do help their organization to move together as one. Core values reflect what's truly important to an organization's stakeholders. They echo a nonprofit's culture and play an important role in advancing the mission. Think of core values as the glue that holds together great organizations. They drive decisions and provide a compass for direction.

Examples of core values include excellence, innovation, quality, caring, diversity, and access. Creating core values defines your nonprofit's character and involves identifying the essence of what your organization does and how you work together to succeed.

Determining your core values requires understanding what your nonprofit stands for and the principles that guide your organization's daily work. Everyone in the organization must be committed to the core values. Nonprofits that remain focused on their values inch closer each day to achieving their vision.

Chapter 8

Shaping Messages that Stick

There is one thing stronger than all the armies in the world, and that is an idea whose time has come.
— Victor Hugo

Messages are everywhere. At movie theaters. Under bridges and down grocery store aisles. In bathrooms and atop buildings. On billboards and buses. We get them when we wake up and they follow us to bed. We even think about them in our sleep. Every day, we are overwhelmed by thousands of messages.

Emails. Voicemails. Postcards. Ads. Texts. And tweets. As the Grinch grumbled, "All the noise, noise, noise, noise!" Getting your message across is harder than ever. Fortunately, the brain acts like a powerful filter that blocks or dismisses unwanted messages and responds to relevant ones.

So how do we break through the clutter? Write effective messages using the right combination of words, often supported by imagery, that resonate with stakeholders. Evoke stored information in the brain. Tap into emotions.

Media theorist Tony Schwartz called this striking a "responsive chord." The late Schwartz was known for his controversial "daisy ad" that ran only once during the 1964 presidential race but changed the course of future political advertising. He believed the goal of messaging was not to introduce new ideas, but to connect with ones already in the mind.

In their classic marketing book, *"Positioning: The Battle for Your Mind,"* Al Ries and Jack Trout note the idea is not to create something new and different, but to manipulate what's already in the brain. For nonprofits, it means connecting with people's past experiences, emotions, and closely held values that have meaning.

For years, researchers have known that the more targeted and individualized public health messages are, the stronger their impact. A 2011 University of Michigan smoking cessation study underscores this theory. Tailored messages have a higher capacity to curb unhealthy behavior. Certainly, "one-size fits all" messages will not connect with everyone and few nonprofits have the budget to create customized marketing packages, although social marketing and microblogging have helped to provide an affordable platform for customization. With a clear understanding of your audience, their needs and wants, your nonprofit can craft core and audience-specific messages that connect with many people on a personal level.

Nonprofits are naturally in the business of "doing good" and messages that appeal to our sense of humanity and making the world a better place may have a better chance of getting through the gateway of our selective mind – at least initially. But whether your message has what it takes to inspire action depends on how well you communicate what people care about in their lives.

Creating Apt Messages

Why do some messages work better than others? What makes them stand out in our mind? Do they possess common characteristics that maximize recall?

I believe message development should be a fun process. So whenever I conduct a creative brainstorming session, I like to warm up the group with famous messages drawn from politics and popular movies. It gets people to open up their minds so words later flow to the surface freely.

Remember these political gems?

- "It's the economy, stupid." (1992 Bill Clinton campaign)
- "Read my lips, no more taxes." (1988 Republican Convention, George Bush)

And who can forget these famous movie one-liners?

- "Do you understand the words coming out of my mouth?" (Rush Hour, 1998)
- "Go ahead. Make my day." (Dirty Harry, 1971)
- "What we have here is a failure to communicate." (Cool Hand Luke, 1967)

These messages entertain us. They are memorable. They stick. They communicate and are clear and understandable. And they are targeted to a specific audience – in this case voters and filmgoers.

In the nonprofit world, message making is both art and science. The goal is to develop language that informs, influences, and inspires action. Apt messages are creative, yet formulated on sound research, testing, strategy, and the ability to communicate effectively with target audiences.

Tips for Effective Message Development

Set your goals. What do you want your message to achieve? Is it to raise funds, describe your organization, or attract volunteers? Most messages are designed to inform, engage, motivate, persuade, or entertain us. They should have impact. They may even save lives.

Know your audience. What makes it tick? What are its demographics? What will your audience find interesting? Know the people you need to reach and understand their needs.

Segment and connect. Every nonprofit should have a set of core messages that overviews the organization and why it exists? In addition, develop customized messages that drill down another level. Segment your audiences and your messages will resonate better.

Keep it simple. People are busy. And they already are inundated with information. Cut through the clutter by keeping your messages short and crisp. Use as few words as possible and make the language understandable. Clarity counts.

Paint a picture. Our minds are hard-wired to process messages in visual ways. Use vivid language that conjures up an image in the mind. For example, it might be "feeding the hungry, preparing youth for college," or "living the American dream."

Be relevant. Craft messages that resonate with your audience. Connect with them using words and key phrases that are meaningful. Plug into their belief system. Think carefully about what you are saying and how it might be perceived by your intended audience.

Evoke emotions. Nonprofit messages that get in touch with feelings work best. Words that connect with us on an emotional level receive the most attention.

Test for success. It's important to test messages with audiences to determine whether they hit the mark. Conduct a small focus group or an online survey to gauge the efficacy of your message. Refine your message when you find it's not working.

Use different media. Messages are delivered across multiple communications channels. Select mediums that make sense for the intended audience based on your message. Take your messages to your audience where they are likely to listen and respond.

Play it again Sam. Repeat your message over and over again. Create a consistency and it will stick in the minds of your audience.

According to the 2011 Edelman Trust Barometer, 59 percent of informed publics aged 25 to 64 years need to see a message three to five times before they believe the information is true.

Refine and perfect. Adjust your messages when you find they are not working. It's important they remain fresh and accurate.

Chapter 9

Multicultural Communications
for Nonprofits

A nation's culture resides in the hearts and in the soul of its people.
– Mohandas Gandhi

By 2050, the racial and ethnic populations of the United States will surpass 50 percent, according to U.S. Census figures. The population speaking a language other than English at home increased by 140 percent during the past three decades. Today, more than 20 million Americans speak poor English and 10 million speak none. More than 300 languages are spoken in America.

Nonprofit organizations, government agencies, and businesses will be challenged to meet growing needs and demands for an increasingly diverse society. Taking a multicultural approach to communication will help your organization remain relevant.

Effective delivery of communication hinges on the target audience's ability to understand messages that inform and influence their decisions. Cultural competency is central to changing behavior, inspiring action, and connecting with people in ways that matter to them. Nonprofits seeking improved relationships, better dialogue, increased support, and greater participation will identify local diversity needs and reach out to those communities and stakeholders.

Over the years, I have had the privilege of working with a variety of nonprofits, government agencies, and businesses engaged in multicultural communications. I learned from those experiences that organizational approaches to building relationships with ethnic and minority populations vary. Success, however, consistently begins with a focus on culture and removing barriers to communication, whether they are language or access related. Each one of us has cultural roots and our own life experiences. Yet we all communicate and share hopes and dreams.

In 1963, during his commencement address on world peace at American University, President John F. Kennedy astutely observed, "...Our most basic common link is that we all inhabit this small planet. We all breathe the same air. We all cherish our children's future. And we are all mortal."

I will never forget running marathons in Baltimore, Philadelphia, and Pittsburgh and how everyone from very diverse neighborhoods and backgrounds cheered us on, offering food, high fives, and kind words of encouragement. It's what makes America's cities and small towns unique and so great.

Recognize that we are all different, but we are also one people. This is the essence of effective nonprofit communications. Nonprofits that can communicate their message cross-culturally will gain broader audience acceptance. How well your message is received and adapted depends on its cultural context and its relevance to the individual in their real world.

Consider these four basic principles that form the Circle of Multicultural Communications, with culture at its center.

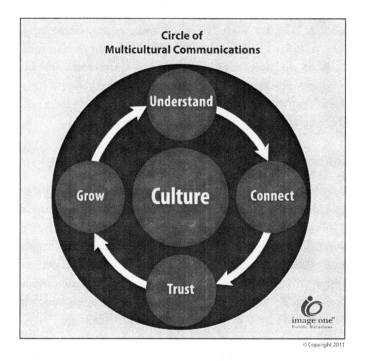

1) **Understand**

Connect with stakeholders by understanding them. Expand your cultural lens. See the world through the eyes of your audience. Walk in their shoes. Review demographic information, including consumer buying and media consumption habits, reading levels, educational backgrounds, health data, and lifestyle decisions. Search for similar needs, characteristics, and preferences. Note: the 2010 Census shows an increasingly diverse U.S. population, including 16% Hispanics, 13% African Americans, 5% Asians, and 1% American Indians and Alaska Natives. Multicultural markets represent approximately 30 percent of the U.S. population.

Know how ethnic and minority populations perceive and interact with your organization. Learn the history of the communities that your nonprofit serves. What are the voting patterns? And who are the community movers and shakers?

Become familiar with the traditions, values, heritage, family dynamics, religious beliefs, and social environment of your audience. What issues do they care about most? Gain audience insights through formative research and community engagement. Stay close to stakeholders who live in the community. Knowing your audience will help you to better communicate with it.

2) Connect

Based on your budget and the importance of reaching a specific audience, develop an outreach plan. Use research and findings to craft strategies and messages that resonate with your target audience. Test your messages for relevance. Hire certified translators and interpreters if necessary. Create publications and other communication products in the appropriate language and dialect. Consider the reading level of your audience. Be sensitive to color selections, shapes, and symbols. Select words that have meaning in the native language.

Whenever possible, connect with stakeholders in their everyday environment. Take your message directly to the streets and the communities that your organization serves. Engage community leaders and influencers to help get the word out. Hold an open house and sponsor community events inviting stakeholders to start a dialog with your nonprofit.

Think about the mediums and ways in which your audience receives information. Review the latest consumption habits for ethnic media that serve your target audience. Identify effective communication channels that present the best opportunity to hold conversations and connect with your target audience.

3) Trust

Form a positive relationship with people by earning their trust. Be a good listener. Respect culture and tradition. Know the protocols and nuisances of working with diverse populations within their community.

Establish a track record of success by consistently delivering on your mission and promise. Communicate often and stay connected to the community. Invite participation and be responsive. Keep up with the latest issues and trends affecting your target audiences.

4) Grow

Mutually rewarding relationships grow. They get stronger over time and result in a win-win for everyone. Successful multicultural communications takes commitment and resources. It's not a one-time deal. It's a continuous learning curve that requires adjustments.

There will be obstacles, but don't let a single failure derail you. Keep your eyes on the horizon and remember why you engaged in multicultural communication in the first place. Nonprofits that achieve a degree of success will be better positioned to serve the unique needs of an increasingly diverse population in America.

Chapter 10

When Web Content Works

Innovation distinguishes between a leader and a follower.
– Steve Jobs

The web is not a kid anymore. It has slowly but surely grown up, and maturity seems to have added greater discipline, efficiency, and personality to a medium that gets more popular everyday. That's the good news for the next generation of websites.

Designers are doing a better job of blending substance with style and sites are now easier to navigate than they were a decade ago. Logins and checkouts have improved and are generally more reliable. So are the tools and software for making online donations.

Nonprofits, too, understand how important it is to align their organizational goals with user goals. The result is more websites that fully brand the organization, while giving users what they want. Nonprofits need to clearly and quickly convey what they stand for and how donations are used to advance the mission.

First Impressions Count

Today, we are bombarded with information and people make decisions about your website in mere seconds. So it's important that the design and content empowers and entertains users. Make sure that your site is appealing and content rich. That means your site colors and images must work in harmony with your messages. Using the right choice of colors can have a big impact on the impression your site makes.

Use color schemes that enhance your site and its content. Visitors respond to colors and visual elements on a psychological level. Making the appropriate color choices can help to express your site's personality and values. Depending on your culture and past experiences, color can put you in the giving mood or create the wrong perception of your organization. Colors should reflect your nonprofit brand, but think carefully about how you use color combinations.

Try to limit your color schemes to two or three complementary colors and small accents of color can be added for highlighting or attention grabbing. Images and photographs can help tell your story in ways that words often can't. The key is balance. Do everything in moderation. Of course, content is still king.

Because reading online content makes us uncomfortable, short sentences and paragraphs work best. Web usability expert Jakob Nielsen has done extensive research on this subject. People simply read online content more slowly than they do from paper.

Use Bold Headlines, Subheads

To reach web audiences, use headlines, subheads, and bullets to highlight text. Write meaningful headlines. Bulleted lists help slowdown the reader's eye, draw attention, and make content easier to scan. Underlined text is usually reserved specifically for links. In addition, limit your use of ALL CAPS and *italics*, which are both considered harder for the eye to decipher.

Keep it Short and Scrollable

Web users will scroll to access copy they need, but don't make them work harder. Keep your page content concise or you will lose them, as they say, in a "New York minute." Use inverted pyramid style in your writing. This means placing the most important information at the top of the page. Use short sentences that keep the reader flow going.

Chunk Your Content

Write your web copy in chunks. Break your text into segments or paragraphs of less than 75 words each. Studies show that chunking copy improves the user's comprehension and content recall. Use each chunk to convey only one idea. This keeps your content focused. Active voice works best. Eliminate all unnecessary words and sentences. Communicate relevance and credibility.

Use Reader Friendly Fonts

Font preferences have remained fairly consistent since the birth of the web. San serifs, such as Verdana and Arial, are easier to read online than Serif text, such as Times New Roman. This is because the shape of Serif letters is more complex and can't be truly replicated with a limited computer screen resolution. Headers and other display text can be more varied. Font sizes should not be too large or small, and can be adjusted according to your audience need and preference.

Black text with a white background works well, but black or dark text with a muted yellow, light gray, or blue background works, too. Just be careful that you have sufficient contrast so reading is easy on the eyes. Leave lots of white space to enhance readability. Try reducing word counts on your pages to 200 words or less. This helps speed up scanning. Also, consider the online needs of people with disabilities.

Proof Your Pages

Check your content for grammar and spelling. Your copy should be error free. If visitors to your site find careless mistakes, they will quickly get the wrong impression about your organization. Run your text through spell check and have an online editor, proofreader, or another person carefully read your content. When you are all done, you will have web content that works. Simplicity and style are in. The best sites attract and retain readers. They keep them coming back for more.

PART IV

Promoting Good Causes

Chapter 11

Media Relations in a Web 2.0 World

The medium is the message.
– Marshall McLuhan

Media relations has changed significantly in just a few short years. Today, it involves far more than sending out news releases and pitching stories. In the Web 2.0 world, there are new rules of engagement.

For the first time, more people said they got news from the web than from newspapers, according to the State of the News Media 2011 report produced by the Pew Research Center's Project for Excellence in Journalism. News content is moving online. People feel increasingly comfortable getting some form of news from the internet, emails, posts, blogs, and social media.

Meanwhile, newsrooms are smaller than they were a decade ago. Many news organizations have died or consolidated. These days many journalists have more duties and are not only reporters, writers, and editors, but also bloggers and social media specialists. Understand that news generation and consumption is increasingly a shared experience. Social media has created more venues for story development and placement. Simultaneously, organizations and journalists have less control over the message.

Traditionally, journalists decided what is or is not news. There were few vehicles for immediate feedback and audience interaction.

h new and social media, user-generated content or "citizen
sm" has opened the door to more two-way communication.
Citizen journalism allows people to use new and social media to
contribute to stories or report live news that might otherwise go
unreported. It might be a digital photo on Flickr, a video streaming
posted to YouTube, or a tweet of some real-time event. Realize that
social media can influence the impact and reach of your story.

While original reporting still packs a powerful punch, technology
has made it possible for greater participation in the story creation
process. Nonprofits interested in extending their media message
should tap into both traditional and new media opportunities.
Cultivate relationships with a broad spectrum of news contacts,
including print and online reporters, editors, freelance writers,
bloggers, and streaming webcast producers.

The New Media Landscape

So what does the new media landscape look like and what are
its implications for nonprofit communicators? Today, effective media
relations requires an "on the street knowledge" of the media and how
and why audiences access news and information. Why do consumers
prefer one medium over another and how will it shape the future
direction of news and media outreach?

In the digital space, news organizations are adjusting to rapidly
changing technologies and consumers who demand news when and
where they want it. For example, according to the Pew Research
Center's 2011 State of the Media, news is going mobile. Nearly half
of all American adults (47 percent) report that they get at least some
local news and information on their cell phone or tablet computer.
So it's likely that media outlets will turn more focus to local news
coverage, which may be a plus for community-based nonprofits.

The Real-Time News Cycle

Ever since cable news arrived in the early 1980s, the 24-hour news cycle has put enormous pressure on media organizations to be first. Today, with the advent of social media, blogs, and streaming video, news is now virtually available in real time. News can go viral almost instantly. History can unfold before our very eyes.

However, attention spans are short. Today's news becomes old fast. Good stories will still find their way into the news cycle, but to be part of a national story, nonprofits need to be proactive and ready to pounce when opportunities arise. Timing makes all the difference in story placement. And what makes headlines in traditional press may not in blogs and social media. This is why it's important for nonprofits to pay attention to relevant and potential stories of interest across multiple media channels.

Another trend is the erasing of lines between blogs and social media. Bloggers' use of and engagement with social media is expanding, as noted in Technorati's 2010 State of the Blogosphere. So as the mediums converge, online news stories and blog posts will increasingly find their way into social networks. In essence, stories will travel across many platforms magnifying their potential influence.

In the Web 2.0 environment, media relations is not a hit or miss game. Success requires staying on top of the issues, listening, and sticking with a strategic and proactive plan. Take media relations seriously and you will achieve increased stakeholder engagement and awareness that raises your nonprofit's profile.

A Media Relations Plan with Traction

Nonprofits often generate compelling news, sometimes more than they know, but due to time constraints and limited budgets have not made it a priority to get the word out. Make a commitment and find resources. Good story placements (earned media) can attract volunteers, raise donations, and increase stakeholder trust.

Nonprofits engaged in active media relations primarily focus their energies on raising their profile or increasing awareness tied to a specific campaign. In both cases, it's important to work from a proactive media relations plan that provides focus and purpose.

Key plan elements include a primary goal, objectives, target audiences, media channels, strategy, news hooks, media evaluation, and messages that maximize opportunities for local and national story placement. Here are eight basic steps for planning and executing an effective media campaign.

Step 1: Determine your goal and campaign objectives. What do you want to accomplish and why? Start with solid research and planning. Do your homework and gather market intelligence. Review existing outreach strategies as a baseline for where you want to go. What is your primary goal? Is it to boost brand awareness, inspire action, further understanding of what your organization does, or garner support for a worthy cause?

Identify measurable objectives that support achievement of your primary goal. For example, your organization may seek to:

- Generate 50 million net positive earned media impressions in a media plan year.
- Increase media coverage annually by 15 percent.
- Secure media coverage in a dozen trade publications.
- Establish regular contact with 25 bloggers and online journalists.

Step 2: Define your budget and timeline. The budget will drive the scope of the campaign and the timeline will keep you on track. Keep your schedule flexible to allow for variations in the news cycle and changing priorities.

Step 3: Know your target audiences. What are the demographics? It may include teens, tweens, moms, seniors, parents, educators, or professionals. It really depends on your campaign and mission. Conduct an analysis of each target audience.

What are the media channels (radio, television, print, social media, etc.) most used by the target audience? When and how often do they use media? Know that media are far more fragmented today and people get their information from a variety of sources.

Access the latest media usage statistics to learn how audiences get news. Turn to annual media analysis reports from leading media research firms, including The Nielsen Company, Vocus, Pew Internet & American Life Project, Arbitron, and the American Press Institute. Many of these research reports are free or available at a minimal cost.

Several common audiences germane to nonprofits include:

- Volunteers and supporters.
- Membership.
- Elected officials.
- Donors and partners.
- Community leaders and influencers.

Step 4: Develop your strategy and tactics. What is your strategy for connecting with media? Three strategies that will help you formulate a robust media plan include:

1) **Identify and Seize Opportunities.** Be ready to pounce on trends and national news stories as they become available. Media opportunities may be tied to timely news events, trends, hot issues, special events, or fresh story angles. This gives you a legitimate platform to pitch reporters. Because of the evolving nature of news, opportunities may change from week to week and month to month. This will require

frequent monitoring, adjustments in the media plan, and matching your stories with what's making news. Other opportunities may arise in responding to news stories and issues with letters to the editor or op-eds.

2) **Cultivate Media.** An important component of any media strategy is the long-term process of cultivating media relationships through periodic calls with reporters and editors. This, in time, will help to plant seeds with reporters who in the future may contact your organization as an expert news source for a story. Sending out monthly news releases to reporters and others who focus on news relevant to your organization will also help to constantly put your organization in front of reporters.

3) **Distribute Timely and Newsworthy Information.** It's vital that your media strategy focus on distributing timely and newsworthy information. This will be key to successful placement. "Old news is no news." Reporters need to receive timely story angles and news releases so they can make accurate news judgments and conduct necessary research for the story as well. Story angles and news hooks, too, need to contain newsworthy and compelling information at the top. Emphasis should be on crafting angles and hooks that strike an emotional chord and are entertaining. Strong visuals or photos should also accompany news releases when possible.

In addition, create tailored short and long-term strategies that reflect the specific objectives of your campaign. Along with your strategies, develop media outreach tactics that advance your goal and objectives.

Step 5: Select media channels. Will your campaign target users of traditional media or social networks or both? What media present the best opportunity to reach your audience staying within your budget and timeline? Armed with knowledge of your key audiences, select your media channels, which may include:

- National media.
- U.S. metro dailies.
- Local print, online, and broadcast outlets.
- Trade press.
- E-newsletters and influential blogs.
- Freelance journalists.

Step 6: Craft your messages. Look for timely news hooks. Keep up with local and national news coverage to find the best story angles. Reporters try to engage their audiences with interesting, unique, and newsworthy stories. Any story that stands out has a solid chance of getting some media attention. Surveys generated by your nonprofit might also make interesting news. Think carefully about framing your messages so they help you achieve your goal. Keep your messages clear, simple, and concise. Keep in mind that you are also writing for diverse mediums and you can't control how your message will be used or if it will be used at all.

Step 7: Execute the plan. With a blueprint in place, it's time to put your strategies and tactics to work. In this stage, based on your plan, you will be writing and distributing news releases, sharing your messages across social media channels, pitching reporters, developing media lists and press kits, responding to media inquiries, placing stories, and building relationships with reporters, editors, and bloggers.

Because news organization turnover is high today, consider investing in an online media database, especially if you are conducting outreach regularly and beyond your local market. Online media databases typically provide thousands of current media contacts nationwide. Several popular news distribution sources include PR Newswire, BurrellesLuce, PR Web, Vocus, Black PRWire, and Hispanic PRWire.

Step 8: Evaluate. Track your results. Are your messages working? Do they need tweaking? Did you meet your goal and objectives? What is your return on investment? Conduct online searches for news. Sign up for Google Alerts. A variety of vendors can help you measure media outcomes and monitor social media for conversations.

Leveraging Media Relations Tools

Here are several proven media relations tools that can help you to achieve your nonprofit's media relations goal and objectives. There are many more.

Traditional Release. Now more than a century old, news releases still work, despite those calling for their demise. The key is writing short releases (less than 400 words) that tell compelling stories. In your email, grab attention with short, catchy subject lines. Your headline needs to tell your story in 12 words or less. Media Advisories or Alerts are separate from news releases and provide a concise, one-page summary of an event, providing the who, what, when, where, and why.

Social Media Release. A relatively new tool is the Social Media Release (SMR) or the Multimedia News Release (MNR), depending on what you call it. These online news releases are format friendly to social media users in the Web 2.0 environment. They serve bloggers and online journalists seeking media rich content. SMRs or MNRs typically include a striking headline, a short introductory paragraph, bulleted lists of facts, unique quotes, a short description of the organization, contact information, links to multimedia (such as video that can be embedded), photographs, and related links.

These social media friendly news releases also increase search engine marketing. Make your subject line short and compelling. Write in inverted pyramid style so the most important information is loaded at the top of the release. Search engines often spider the first 300 to 500 words. Press releases with multimedia elements generate up to 77 percent more views than text-only releases, according to 2011 PR Newswire analysis. You can distribute SMRs or MNRs through newswire services, such as PR Newswire. The National Restaurant Association is an example of a nonprofit that has distributed SMRs.

Video News Release. In the age of YouTube and Internet TV, an online Video News Release (VNR) gives nonprofits an opportunity to distribute packaged news and information in a visually appealing way. You can go viral fast by sharing your content across video sharing networks. Seven out of 10 adult internet users have used the internet to watch or download video, according to the 2010 State of Online Video report prepared by the Pew Internet and American Life Project.

Your story can be presented as a single episode or as a short series known as Webisodes. Online videos are also included as links in social media releases and shared across social media networks. With the explosion of more than 300 video sharing sites, the online VNR presents a cost-effective tool for nonprofits to get the word out.

Audio News Release and Radio Media Tour. Radio is still one of the most popular and effective ways of communicating your nonprofit message. The Audio News Release (ANR) is a sound release that is packaged specifically for radio. It may actually be the audio component of a video news release.

The ANR, which is a broadcast audio file, is distributed and pitched to radio stations and networks. You can also line up a series of back-to-back radio interviews featuring your spokesperson through a Radio Media Tour (RMT). Tobin Communications, Inc., News Generation, and Strauss Radio Strategies are examples of firms that can help you to set up an RMT for a fee. RMTs are often setup for the morning drive time.

Exclusive. Granting an exclusive means you are agreeing to let a journalist break a story first before other news organizations. Some media outlets won't run a story at all without an exclusive. Other media outlets don't care. Offer an exclusive only when you believe that you are sitting on a newsworthy story with high national or special interest. Focus on a media outlet that will give your nonprofit the biggest bang.

Weigh the costs of a single placement versus potentially less coverage across multiple news sources. I believe exclusives are worth it when you can land a key outlet, such as a major network, the *Wall Street Journal, USA Today*, or another media outlet that has a strong connection to your target audience. Influential bloggers linked to powerful social networks may work just as well. Be clear about expectations and what you are getting for offering an exclusive.

Embargo. Journalists often like to get news and information ahead of time, especially if they have long lead times, or prefer doing additional research and original reporting. Daily newspapers, for instance, require less lead time than a monthly magazine, although online editions and social networks help to eliminate this challenge. Use an embargo when you want to strategically time when news actually hits the street.

An embargo means you are providing the information to the journalist before you actually want the story to break. Most journalists will honor the understanding that they will not go with the story until the official release date. Be very clear about the official release date and time, including the time zone.

Media kit. Journalists still like getting quality press kits that contain timely and useful information for a story. Create print and online versions. Elements of a press kit include a folder, introductory letter, a news release, a fact sheet, backgrounders, recent news coverage, and biographical information. Provide access to the materials, including multimedia products, presentations, and photos, via your online newsroom or a custom URL. Include keywords and tags to enhance search engine optimization.

The advantage of online press kits is they allow you to do Web analytics and can be instantly available to journalists everywhere. Print versions of media kits are popular with journalists who actually like opening their mail.

News conference. In the age of online journalism and shrinking newsrooms, press conferences have lost some of their effectiveness. It's really hard these days to pull reporters away from their desk. They just don't have the time. You must have something significant to say, such as a major campaign launch or a high-level announcement. Without an exceptional news hook, no one will show up. Pick a location for your press conference that has news appeal and provides easy access for reporters. Early mornings and afternoons present the best time to hold your event. Make sure broadcast media have a place to plug in their satellite feeds and equipment.

Start the conference promptly, provide press kits, and hold a short question and answer period at the end. In your advance news release or media alert, let reporters know if post photo or interview opportunities will be made available.

Opinion pieces. Write an op-ed when you want to convey a viewpoint that aligns with your mission. Be timely and relevant. Support your case with facts and say something original. Paint a picture. Present a fresh angle that sparks reader interest. Most op-eds are between 500 and 700 words. Follow the submission guidelines of the target publication to increase your chance of success. Realize that op-ed placement is difficult and success is inconsistent but rewarding when it happens.

Public service announcements. You might say public service announcements (PSAs) are a nonprofit's best friend. They are the perfect awareness building tool for nonprofits and government agencies that have an important public message to share – whether it's preventing forest fires, preparing for disasters, or promoting healthier lives. Traditional PSA topics focus on safety and health but others are welcome. PSAs can communicate a vital message, while also helping stations to fill unsold air time or advertising space.

Broadcast PSAs are designed for radio, television, and cable distribution. Their lengths vary, but are normally 15, 30, or 60 seconds, depending on the station requirements. Either ready-to-air or text versions may be distributed. Print PSAs, which often complement broadcast PSA campaigns, also play an important role in influencing target audiences. Include your call to action. Be creative and track coverage. You can produce PSAs in-house or hire outside help depending on your budget. The Ad Council has supported thousands of public service campaigns on behalf of nonprofits and government agencies and may be a potential resource for your organization. Visit www.adcouncil.org for more information on campaign selection criteria.

Letters to the Editor. These short pieces are sent to print publications in response to a story, to critique an article, or to highlight an issue. This media relations tool gives nonprofits an opportunity to express their concern, present ideas, or offer solutions. Keep your letter short and stay on message. Read the publication guidelines carefully for proper submission. News space is tight so don't be disappointed if your letter is not published. However, published letters are a valued placement as many influencers and advocates read them.

Online commenting. Posting comments to online stories and blogs gives nonprofits a chance to present their perspective of the story. You may also note errors or points of omission. It also continues the dialogue and lets journalists and bloggers know you are reading their stuff. Keep your comments short and professional.

Online pressroom. Make a journalist's job easier by developing and maintaining an online pressroom on your website. The interactive page should include media contact information, news releases, your e-press kits, facts, biographical information, photos, links to your social media pages, and hot topics. Provide Really Simple Syndicate (RSS) feed options and the ability to sign up to receive e-newsletters. Keep your online newsroom fresh and relevant.

Working with Media

As a former newspaper reporter, I have an appreciation for the job of a journalist. Over the years, I've also enjoyed getting fresh perspectives on today's proper media manners. The success of any media strategy hinges largely on building relationships and trust with journalists. Here are several tips for cultivating relationships with journalists.

- **Be prepared.** When a reporter calls, be ready to respond. Always have a nearby list of key talking points and messages. Have your facts straight, listen carefully, and gain an understanding of what the story is about and what the reporter needs.
- **Stick to the facts.** Don't exaggerate and stay on message. Don't speculate. Honesty and accuracy is always the best policy for working with journalists.
- **Respect reporters.** Journalists are very busy people. Respect their time. Never lose your cool or argue with a media representative. Treat reporters as you would want to be treated yourself.
- **Be responsive.** Reporters operate on tight deadlines and often need information quickly. Never ignore phone calls or be evasive. Answer media calls within an hour if possible.
- **Answer directly and follow-up.** Sometimes you get asked a question that you don't have an immediate answer for, at least initially. Tell the reporter you will get back to them with a response as soon as possible. Ask for the reporter's deadline.

Never try to guess, as it will only lead to inaccuracies. Get it right the first time.

Raising Visibility: Lutheran Services in America

Online auctions can raise big bucks for big causes and are a popular fundraising tool for nonprofits. Almost as importantly, they can generate buzz and boost a nonprofit's national visibility. Lutheran Services in America (LSA) and its online charity, Trading Graces, is the perfect example.

LSA is one of the largest nonprofit networks in the United States and is an alliance of the Evangelical Lutheran Church in America, the Lutheran Church-Missouri Synod, and their more than 300 related health and human services organizations. Together, these organizations touch the lives of more than six million people – one in 50 Americans each year.

In 2005, LSA kicked off its first Trading Graces online auction during the holiday season and worked closely with Image One PR to spread the word. The story angle centered on regifting. "What do you do with holiday gifts you really don't want and can't return? Try regifting them for a real cause – charity. It's the perfect solution for gift overload." The media nibbled at the news hook.

ABC World News Tonight was looking for a holiday story and Trading Graces fit the bill. LSA President Jill Schumann delivered an excellent television interview and the auction gained fast national attention, helping to generate 18 million media impressions and 2 million hits to the LSA website. The story was also covered by PBS, Washington Post, Washington Times, Baltimore Sun, Philadelphia Daily News, Chronicle of Philanthropy, NonProfit Times and earned broadcast coverage in more than a dozen local television stations nationwide. The media campaign won two Silver Communicator

Awards in the National Media Campaign and Single Placement categories.

"Lutheran Services in America was early to the online auction field and was able to turn that into image-raising for Lutheran health and human services as well as fund raising for participating member organizations," said LSA Director of Communications Jeanean Merkel.

Trading Graces proceeds benefited Lutheran health and human services organizations. Items were donated locally and auctioned online on eBay. The auction was hosted by MissionFish, which is eBay's charity support division. A follow-up media campaign in 2006, combined with a series of radio public service announcements, resulted in approximately 16 million media impressions, including airing in hundreds of local radio stations.

In 2010, buyers and sellers on eBay, the world's leading e-commerce marketplace, donated $54.8 million to United States and United Kingdom nonprofit organizations. A donation was made every 24 seconds through eBay Giving.

In 2010, Bidding For Good celebrated crossing over the $100 million milestone in funds raised to support nonprofits and schools in America. Bidding For Good hosted 3,444 auctions in 2010 with gross merchandise sales of $33.8 million.

Proactive Versus Reactive PR

Practicing proactive public relations will help your nonprofit avoid always responding in the reactive mode. It's a lot like preventive medicine. "An apple a day keeps the doctor away." Staying in front of issues is challenging. It requires doing your homework and taking the initiative.

Following a proactive philosophy does not, however, have to cost a lot. Sometimes it's as simple as picking up the phone or writing and distributing a press release. The problem is not enough nonprofits make the commitment of time and resources.

A Checklist for Proactive PR

- ☐ Does your nonprofit routinely send out news releases about positive stories?
- ☐ Does your nonprofit take the initiative and maintain a regular dialogue with local, national, and specialty media?
- ☐ Does your organization respond immediately to inaccurate facts or perceptions portrayed by the media?
- ☐ Does your organization brainstorm for ideas to highlight goodwill and success?
- ☐ Does your nonprofit routinely communicate with Congress and other policy influencers?
- ☐ Does your nonprofit periodically survey members and service recipients for perceptions?
- ☐ Does your nonprofit research, plan, and evaluate public relations efforts?
- ☐ Does your nonprofit have a crisis communication plan in place?

Your Crisis Communications Plan

You've heard it before. Always expect the unexpected. Emergency responders encourage us to be ready for when disaster strikes. Don't wait until a crisis happens. Plan now. Be prepared.

Have a crisis communications plan and policy in place. It will help you to mitigate risks and guide your nonprofit through troubled waters. Start by establishing a clearly defined channel of communication. Answer these critical questions for effective response.

- ▪ Who in your organization will be part of the crisis response team?
- ▪ Do you have an emergency contact tree with office and mobile phone numbers?

- Who will handle media inquiries?
- Who will act as your nonprofit spokesperson(s)?
- How will messages be developed and disseminated?
- Has your spokesperson(s) received media training?

When a crisis occurs, put your plan into action. Call your crisis response team to order and assess the situation. Does the crisis impact public perception? Are their financial ramifications? Decide a course of action that includes timely release of information to the media and public.

Verify facts and act swiftly. Maintain control. Address your key messages. Repeat facts and ensure the reporter understands you clearly to avoid being misquoted.

Monitor media and public response. Evaluate your outcomes. Will your organization bounce back quickly and did you maintain public trust? Record lessons learned and examine ways your nonprofit can improve response to future crises. Review your crisis communications plan annually, update your contact tree frequently, and evaluate the potential types of crises that may affect your organization.

Giving Media Interviews

Your nonprofit has just kicked off a major public awareness campaign and you are beginning to get calls from the media. Television, radio, and newspaper reporters are interested in your story and want an interview. Is your executive director or spokesperson up to the challenge?

Here are several media training tips that will help your spokespersons to get the most out of their interview opportunities.

Be Prepared. Some of us are just naturally better speakers and adept at giving presentations and interviews. But even the most polished executives prepare in advance. Research the topic of the interview. Is the interview with print or broadcast media? And who is its primary audience? Go over questions that might be asked. Develop compelling sound bites for a strong response. Do a rehearsal or role playing with colleagues. Practice giving counterpoints to tough questions.

Be in Control. Go into your interview relaxed, poised, and ready for an engaging conversation. Talk to the interviewer and not the camera. Stay calm, be confident, and remain focused. Watch your body language and posture. Use your hands to demonstrate certain points. Be energetic but not animated.

Stay on Message. Reporters will sometimes throw you zingers that completely take you off your train of thought. Don't let these challenging questions derail you. Learn how to "bridge" or create transitions that bring the interview back to where it was intended to go in the first place. Bridging phases include:

- "Let me rephrase that a little differently..."
- "That is a good question that I would like to put in perspective..."
- "Before we get off our topic, let me stress one more point..."

Never, however, say "no comment." Instead, deflect the question. "It's not our policy to discuss this specific issue, but I would like to point out..." Or just simply say "I do not have an answer to your question at the moment but we will respond as soon as we have more information." Pause for a few seconds, if needed, to gather your thoughts and deliver effective responses.

Keep it Simple. Whether you are doing a print or broadcast interview, keep your messages short and sweet. Avoid using jargon and make your answers understandable to the average person on the street. Use concrete examples and human stories to illustrate your statements when appropriate. Use poignant facts to support your message points.

Chapter 12

Becoming Word on the Street

I have found that among its other benefits, giving liberates the soul of the giver.
– Maya Angelou

Can nonprofits with small budgets really create big buzz? The answer is a resounding yes and history proves it. The American Red Cross was not always the size and scale it is today. Word of mouth and other public outreach strategies played an important role in the extraordinary growth of the nonprofit organization from 1914-1918.

During this period, the number of Red Cross chapters rose sharply from 107 to 3,864 and Red Cross members grew from 16,708 to more than 20 million. This was achieved in an era without television and radio had not yet became mainstream in America. As more people joined the Red Cross, the faster word about the organization spread throughout communities.

While working at the American Red Cross headquarters in Washington, D.C., I remember learning Red Cross history and seeing a splendid collection of Red Cross posters spanning several decades. The posters, along with word of mouth, The Red Cross magazine, brochures, newspaper advertisements, banners, billboards, public events, speakers, and short films played at movie houses, all created the buzz needed to raise funds, recruit volunteers, and promote the organization during the war.

People with passion for a cause drive word of mouth influence. The credibility of the messenger is vital to success. Recommendations from personal acquaintances or opinions posted by consumers online are the most trusted forms of advertising, according to a Nielsen Global Online Consumer Survey. The 2009 survey of more than 25,000 internet consumers from 50 countries revealed that 90 percent of consumers surveyed noted that they trust recommendations from people they know, while 70 percent trusted consumer opinions posted online.

Based on this personal trust factor, it makes sense for nonprofits to recruit stakeholders, including volunteers, members, and service recipients, to help get the word out. Volunteers who are out on the frontline everyday can be powerful voices for increasing awareness and building support.

The best testimonials, too, often come from stakeholders who care about the organization and have a passion for the cause. Arm your champions with the right messages and create venues for them to communicate with target audiences. Engaging these "influencers" will get word of mouth rolling. Today, word of mouth remains a popular and effective channel for connecting with stakeholders in a meaningful way.

Although word of mouth has long been used to advance causes, including the Civil Rights Movement in America, it has only recently evolved into a formal marketing discipline. The Word of Mouth Marketing Association (WOMMA) was created in 2004. WOMMA is the premier nonprofit organization that advances and advocates for credible word of mouth marketing offline and online. The important message here is to include word of mouth marketing in your communications strategy. Build your contact list and take your message to the streets.

Along with word of mouth, nonprofits engage a variety of strategies and tactics that get people talking about the organization, including posters, postcards, speaking engagements, giveaways, blogs, and special events (fairs, contests, and open houses).

Postcards Still a Good Pitch

Digital marketing is all the talk these days, but direct mail still packs a punch and so do postcards – a great tool for nonprofits looking to get a quick message across in a visually appealing and non intrusive way.

During the height of the dot.com craze, postcards seemed to lose their edge as marketers moved to new forms of online promotion. But today, popup ads and spam are just plain annoying, while targeted postcards get read. Of course, online advertising will continue to rise but consumers are becoming increasingly selective about acceptable forms of online promotion.

Fast, Easy, and Cost Effective

So why is the simple postcard still effective? A postcard can deliver information the way people want it today – fast, easy, and with no hassles. You don't even have to open the envelope. The message is right in front of your face. Postcards also have that personal connection with people. Perhaps, they remind us of those times when we get postcards from family and friends.

Marketers especially like postcards because they are cost effective and easy to produce. The key is ensuring that you have a relevant message and an effective mailing list aimed at your audience. Community nonprofits can do targeted postcards to stakeholders living in the vicinity.

Popular Postcard Pitches

Another advantage to postcards is that they can be created as a single marketing piece or they can be part of a larger promotional effort. Here are several postcard ideas and uses:

- Announce a new website or generate more online traffic.
- Launch a new product or service.
- Encourage attendance at a workshop or special event.
- Celebrate anniversaries.
- Kickoff new campaigns.
- Inform audiences about awards or contests.
- Remind audiences about events or deadlines.

Create Effective Postcards

Postcards that gain attention have a common set of characteristics, yet each card has its own unique creative design. Effective postcards are eye-catching, fun-to-read, and focus on a key message and call to action. Several tips for creating highly effective postcards include:

Keep it Simple. You have 10 seconds or less to capture a reader's interest. It's love at first sight or the trash. Use persuasive language and resist the urge to fill up the postcard with text. Ideally, use no more than 75 words on the entire postcard. Focus on a single important message.

Be Creative. Think of a postcard as a creative canvass. Dare to be different using a powerful photo, illustration, or a cool, yet professional design for the front side of the postcard. Brightly colored postcards grab more attention and encourage more readership than dark and dull postcards.

Make it Timely. Marketing is all about timing. If you are promoting a special event, give the reader at least two weeks advance notice. Many timely postcards are tied to current events.

Create a Postcard Cycle. Today, the average person gets besieged by daily messages and it's getting harder to cut through the clutter. To be heard, many marketers like to create a quarterly or monthly postcard cycle. You can promote your nonprofit brand this way and market different products or services during the cycle. P.S. Postcards Work!

Special Events for the Greater Good

People like to feel they are part of something larger than themselves. They want to actively participate in events and activities that hold personal meaning for them. Nonprofits provide a channel for fulfilling the desire to do good.

Through special events, stakeholders can exercise their passion and commitment to important causes. Creating a national awareness event gives nonprofits an opportunity to rally stakeholder support and build unity, while drawing attention to an important issue, whether it's heart disease, safety, education, or the environment.

The first Earth Day was held on August 22, 1970, which engaged 20 million Americans and is widely credited with launching the modern environmental movement, according to the Earth Day Network. The passage of the landmark Clean Air Act, Clean Water Act, Endangered Species Act, and other groundbreaking environmental laws soon followed.

February is American Heart Month, which puts the spotlight on cardiovascular disease, a leading cause for death of American women and men. April is National Autism Awareness Month observed by the Autism Society since the 1970s.

Did you know that March 30th is National Doctor's Day in America? This event, which celebrates the contributions of physicians, began in 1933 in Winder, Georgia. National Nurses Week begins each May with National Nurses Day. Each September, the American Association of Suicidology observes National Suicide Prevention Week. Since the 1970s, this special event raises national awareness and advances the goals of suicide prevention. The event coincides with World Suicide Prevention Week.

Each year, nonprofits hold hundreds of national awareness days, weeks, and months that raise public consciousness. In 2000, while working for what is now ICF International, I was privileged to have an opportunity to work closely with the U.S. Department of Housing and Urban Development (HUD) to create the first Neighborhood Networks Week.

The national event highlighted the important role that HUD community technology centers play in helping low-income families to bridge the digital divide and become self-sufficient. Over the years, Neighborhood Networks Week events have included live webcasts, poster and essay contests, conference calls, and web chats.

Across the nation, Neighborhood Networks centers have hosted their own local events, such as open houses, grand openings, job fairs, health screenings, safety awareness programs, and community outreach days. These local and national events helped to create a common bond among Neighborhood Networks stakeholders, while raising visibility and garnering support.

Nonprofits seeking a creative way to connect stakeholders and build buzz can develop their own special event unique to the organization and its mission. In planning your event, think carefully about how you will engage audiences while also attracting community and media interest. Timing is critical. Try to avoid competing against other high-profile events held during the same time to maximize the impact of your event. Once you have established a time, keep it the same each year.

Many organizations develop an event planning guide or media kits that provide participants with guidance and promotional ideas. Media outreach suggestions include:

- Contacting the Governor's or Mayor's office to request a special proclamation designated for your event.
- Preparing and distributing Public Service Announcements (PSAs) to community radio and television stations.
- Placing op-eds and letters to the editor.
- Inviting influential speakers.

- Offering interviews to print and broadcast media.

In time, if you keep your special event fresh and interesting, it will take on a life of its own, creating tradition and a popular venue for getting your message out.

The Ancient Art of Storytelling

For thousands of years, the ancient art of storytelling has helped diverse peoples to share their voices and convey important messages. Native Americans, for example, pass down stories from generation to generation as part of their strong oral history and tradition. The stories play an important role in teaching, healing, and in preparing native people for change and adversity.

Nonprofits, too, for centuries have shared success stories that provide tangible proof that their work makes a difference. As brothers Chip and Dan Heath point out in their book, *"Made to Stick,"* nonprofits have long figured out that donors respond better to individuals than to abstract causes.

People relate to real-life stories because they humanize information. Storytelling entertains us and stirs emotions far beyond those brought out by a single message. Storytelling allows nonprofits to communicate their value and return on investment.

While working on HUD's Neighborhood Networks initiative, I wrote dozens of success stories that highlighted remarkable resident achievement. Youth improving their grades and going to college. Adults getting better jobs and buying their first home. And seniors making online connections with family and friends when they had never touched a computer before.

Your organization has many compelling stories that need to be told, too. Here are some tips for good nonprofit storytellers.

- Seek success stories from a variety of sources, including service recipients, volunteers, donors, and staff.
- Keep your stories short and enhance them with photographs. Blend statistics with inspiring stories of individuals that capture the imagination.
- Highlight success stories on your website, in publications, and through social media. Share them with media as well.

Diving into Digital Storytelling

In recent years, with the evolution of new and social media, digital storytelling has become popular in the nonprofit community, especially among organizations that serve youth. Digital storytelling merges the ancient art of storytelling with modern technology. Using computer-based tools, digital storytelling interlaces narrative, voice, music, and images to tell stories. It's an emotionally engaging way to express personal life experiences.

Both traditional and digital forms of storytelling give nonprofits powerful devices for sharing success in creative and entertaining ways.

Outdoor Advertising Larger Than Life

Thousands of years ago, the Egyptians used enormous stones to publicize laws and treaties. Many civilizations later, merchants painted wooden signs and glued gigantic posters to walls and fences to sell remedies and common goods.

And today, with new digital technologies, outdoor advertising can be customized for just about any marketing venue. In 2010, advertisers spent $6.1 billion in outdoor advertising, according to the Outdoor Advertising Association of America, Inc. (OAAA). The five major outdoor advertising categories include cinema, transit, billboard, street furniture, and alternative.

In an increasingly mobile society, outdoor advertising presents nonprofits with a larger than life opportunity to connect with audiences, including potential donors. The outdoor advertising industry has a long tradition of public service dating back before World War I. The industry donates more than $400 million in space and production every year, the OAAA reports.

Local nonprofits and charities can use the OAAA Find a Member tool to identify outdoor advertising companies that may assist them. The OAAA designates a select number of nonprofits as National Public Service Partners. These partners receive operational and promotional support, as well as placement in large, medium, and small markets. Visit OAAA.org for more information.

Remember outdoor advertising is all about telling a story in seconds. Award-winning outdoor designers believe the best ads often project humor, surprise, emotion, culture, and aesthetic value. The most effective ads focus on a single idea and the right concept can generate millions of media impressions that support your cause.

PART V

New and Social Media

Chapter 13

Social Media for Nonprofits

To be social is to be forgiving.
– Robert Frost

Nonprofits understand that engaging in social media is not a choice but a necessity in the Web 2.0 world. The real challenge today for nonprofits is charting the right course for success and demonstrating a return on investment.

According to the 2011 Nonprofit Social Network Benchmark Report, 89% of nonprofits have a presence on Facebook. Usage levels of Twitter, the micro-blogging community, were at 57% in 2011 and LinkedIn is used by 1 in 3 nonprofits (30%). Conducted by NTEN, Common Knowledge, and Blackbaud, the annual survey analyzed responses from 11,196 nonprofit professionals.

Nonprofits have turned the corner in their use of social media, but like many organizations are still figuring out how to maximize their participation and use the right tools effectively. Why are nonprofits using social media? It depends on their goals.

10 Reasons to Engage in Social Media

1) Extend the reach of traditional marketing.
2) Learn what is being said about your organization and relevant issues.
3) Promote new products and services.

4) Encourage event participation.
5) Fundraise and expand campaign support.
6) Share news and other quality content.
7) Raise visibility and reach influencers.
8) Rally support for a cause.
9) Recruit staff and volunteers.
10) Increase web traffic.

The wrong reason to engage in social media is simply because everyone's doing it. Nonprofits that create a solid media strategy, including policies, standards, and usage guidelines for staff, are likely to achieve greater success. A significant challenge is dedicating sufficient resources, expertise, and staff hours to maintain an active presence. Just creating a Facebook page and YouTube channel does not cut it.

Developing Your Strategy

The leap into social media is a big one that requires strategy and organizational commitment. Put social media in the annual budget. Hire dedicated staff if needed. Attend seminars and workshops to stay abreast of the latest trends and techniques.

Social media responsibilities frequently fall under the communications umbrella, but it takes contributions from all departments, including executive leadership. Be clear that social media success requires continuous staff involvement. Don't think of social media as added cost but instead as a tool for increasing communications efficiency and impact.

Your nonprofit may have joined the conversation years ago, or it may be diving in for the first time. Whether you are moving from early adoption to full engagement, develop a realistic strategy with defined goals, objectives, and benchmarks for success. Don't make the mistake of starting a social media campaign and then abandoning it. Keep engaged and post regularly to maintain an active presence.

Remember that social media activities should be a part of your broader marketing plan. Your social media strategy, goal, and objectives should support your total communications effort. For example, by leveraging social media networks you can increase media coverage and raise awareness – which may advance your media relations goals.

Where to begin? Your social media strategy should include a primary goal, supporting objectives, target audiences, a plan of engagement, and measurement. You will also need to create a promotional plan to get the word out about your nonprofit's social media presence and activities. Promotion of your social network community may include the organization's website, emails, events, and advertising.

Monitoring the Social Web

Begin your social media journey by listening and observing. There are several free services that can help your nonprofit to tune into the social web. Realize that monitoring is different than metrics. Monitoring helps you get a pulse on what is being said about your organization and related issues, while metrics actually measure the impact of your social media efforts.

Start by creating a list of key words associated with your nonprofit, including the name of the organization, key leaders, programs, services, and related issues in the news. You will feed these words into search engines. Next, set up a Really Simple Syndication (RSS) reader, such as Google Reader. This online aggregator constantly monitors your preferred news sites and blogs for new content. It displays all of your favorite sites in one place. You can then subscribe to relevant blogs and RSS feeds. Look for the RSS icons. If you have not already done so, add an RSS feed to your website.

Also sign-up for Google Alerts, which are email updates of the latest news and web search results based on your choice of topic or query. This allows you to keep up with developing stories, discussion threads, and industry trends. In addition, Google for Nonprofits offers free or discounted resources, applications, and outreach tools. Services include discounted or free Google apps, free AdWords advertising, premium branding, and increased uploads on YouTube. Google+ provides another social media platform for nonprofits.

Use Twitter Search to track entries in the micro-blogging world. Technorati, too, can help you to track blog mentions and topics germane to your nonprofit. Along with these monitoring services, Vocus can integrate social media coverage with traditional coverage, analyze your online reputation, and monitor more than 20 million of the most influential blogs. PR Newswire also offers commercial monitoring services.

Posting Compelling Content

Part of your social media strategy should focus on how you will consistently develop, collect, and post quality content. This is important for attracting fans and followers. Write about news, topics, and activities that reflect your nonprofit's mission. It should also resonate with stakeholders you want to reach. Quality content is timely, useful, inviting, and conversational. Always be professional and never frivolous. Your content should have purpose and value. Learn the language and nuisances of each social media channel to build a better connection with the audience. Items for posting may include surveys, reports, events, research, milestones, hot topics for discussion, and news. Share your content across all your social media channels.

Measuring Success

Nonprofits that have already taken the plunge into the social web or are experienced performers need to measure their success. Metrics can help you achieve this and track your return on investment (ROI).

Several common measuring sticks include:

- Counting friends, followers, and fans.
- Web traffic and page views.
- Increased awareness.
- Comments and subscribers.
- Donor revenue.

These metrics can be obtained using either free or commercial analytical tools. Facebook Insights gathers metrics around content and usage. Using this tool, you can measure consumption of content, demographic information, and fan interaction. Take time to carefully analyze all information you collect. If you don't have the expertise to accurately assess your social media efforts, hire a consultant. Based on your metrics and monitoring, adapt and adjust your social media strategy accordingly.

Your Facebook and Twitter Communities

Facebook provides nonprofits with an easy to create, update, and manage tool for engaging in the social media web. It's by far the most popular social media service for nonprofits. Facebook instantly connects your organization with more than 800 million active users.

Facebook can help your nonprofit to extend its reach by leveraging visibility across other social media channels. You can also purchase ads to help build your fan base. Facebook Insights is a free service that provides nonprofits with valuable metrics to understand and analyze trends, interaction, user growth, consumption of content, and demographics.

Using Facebook, nonprofits can post photos, organize events, share videos and success stories, raise funds, mobilize stakeholders, and increase awareness. You can even poll your supporters.

In 2011, Facebook launched a new Resource Section that helps nonprofits to maximize their Facebook presence. Resources include tips and best practices for nonprofits, exploring how to integrate Facebook via social plugins, and creating ads.

Since launching with Facebook Platform in 2007, Causes has become the world's largest online destination where individuals come together to engage in philanthropy and activism, according to the Causes.com website. Causes has raised more than $30 million for 25,000 nonprofits since 2007 benefitting over 500,000 member-related causes.

The application allows registered Facebook users to highlight their support of a favorite cause on their profiles. Through Causes Wish on the Cause.com site, users have donated more than $13 million dollars through birthdays, weddings, special events, and holidays. Cause users, of which there are more than 150 million, can encourage their friends to join, donate, or fundraise.

Twitter for Nonprofits

Created in 2006, Twitter is an effective social networking service and microblogging tool that connects nonprofits with millions of potential followers. Each Tweet is up to 140 characters in length and answers the question, "What's happening?" More than one in 10 adults online in the United States uses Twitter, according to a 2011 study from the Pew Internet and American Life Project.

The great thing about Twitter is it forces you to be concise and compelling, while still giving you an opportunity to go deeper. You can tell your story in a headline or use the details pane to share photos, video, and other media content. Twitter can also help your nonprofit to promote events, announce new services, support fundraising, and encourage participation. Use Twitter to gather real-time intelligence and feedback and build relationships with supporters, donors, and potential partners.

Build your followers by offering useful content and insights that support your mission, while adding to the social media conversation. Share news, successes, observations, and Retweets that align with your nonprofit's focus and purpose.

YouTube and Flickr for Nonprofits

The popularity of video and photo sharing continues to grow. More video is uploaded to YouTube in 60 days than the three major U.S. networks created in 60 years. This YouTube fact says a lot about the power and influence of online video content. According to the 2011 Nonprofit Social Network Benchmark Report, nearly half (47%) of charities indicated they have a presence on YouTube.

Creating a YouTube channel offers nonprofits many benefits. You can tell your story in an emotionally appealing video format, connect with stakeholders, reach volunteers, and attract potential donors. YouTube also offers a Nonprofit program for U.S. organizations that have current 501(c)(3) status. Program benefits cited by YouTube include:

- Premium branding capabilities and increased uploading capacity.
- The option to drive fundraising through a Google Checkout "Donate" button.
- Listing on the Nonprofit channel and the Nonprofit video pages.
- Ability to add a Call-to-Action overlay on your videos to drive campaigns.

Flickr for Nonprofits

People love photos and Flickr offers fast access to a dynamic, interactive online community for sharing images and telling stories. Flickr is home to over five billion photos and more than 10 million active groups, according to the company website. Nonprofits can use Flickr for multiple purposes, including highlighting events and success stories. It can also be used as an image library for internal or external photo exchange. You can also create groups and participate in discussions.

So let's say you are creating an annual report and photographers from four different locations are contributing images. Everyone can just login and upload to Flickr to create a collection for viewing and photo selection. Pictures can be easily uploaded to Flickr via the web, mobile, email, or photo applications. Photos in Flickr can also be shared across social media platforms, including Facebook, Twitter, email, and blogs. Tag your images and refresh your collections.

To support nonprofits, Flickr has partnered with Tech Soup, a U.S.-based nonprofit technology resource, to offer free Pro Accounts, which provide significantly more storage and unlimited photo uploads (20MB per photo).

Blogging to Say Something

Blogs have become a widely accepted and influential tool for getting your message across to audiences. As of November 2011, BlogPulse noted more than 177 million public blogs. By 2014, the blog audience is expected to increase to 60 percent of internet users, or 150 million people, according to eMarketer.

As a type of website, often created in WordPress, blogs give nonprofits an online channel for communicating with audiences. You can provide commentary, share insights, announce new initiatives, and highlight events combining text, images, links, and other media.

Tips for Blogging

- Create a blog name that reflects the essence or character of your nonprofit. Make it unique and appealing to potential audiences. Blog when you have something to say. It might be your view on a policy issue, to mark a milestone, or release breaking news. Journalists check blogs regularly for potential news content.

- Keep your blog posts timely and short, usually under 300 words. Use bulleted lists to break up text where possible. Expand your thinking and align your blog posts with your communications strategy. Always be civil, identify yourself, and respond to comments when appropriate. Write engaging blog titles to draw reader interest. Be sure your blog can be easily shared across other social media channels. Along with other social media channels, promote your blog.

Blogging should not be the responsibility of one person at your nonprofit. Encourage other staff, board members, and volunteers to make contributions about relevant and interesting topics. Dedicate adequate staff, resources, and time for blogging. Post regularly and monitor relevant citations in the blogosphere. Use blog search engines, including Technorati, Bloglines, BlogScope, and Google Blog Search, to find updates on the latest blog entries associated with your nonprofit.

The Move to Mobile Marketing

The nation has gone mobile and consumers are increasingly using their mobile devices to do a variety of things, including check the weather, access social media, get news, play games, and purchase merchandise. Nonprofits, too, see the value of connecting with stakeholders using text messaging, whether to provide alerts or garner support. The primary benefit of mobile marketing is the ability to send targeted, highly personal messages to stakeholders.

The fundraising response to natural disaster campaigns, such as the American Red Cross efforts following the Japan and Haiti Earthquakes, has proven the effectiveness of text messaging.

Although mobile marketing has not yet heavily penetrated the nonprofit sector, it will as mobile internet usage rises. So begin adding mobile phone numbers to your contacts database. Morgan Stanley predicts that mobile will be bigger than desktop Internet by 2014. Driven by the Apple iPad, Galaxy Samsung Tab, and other models, sales of tablet computers will continue as well.

So what does this sea change mean for the nonprofit sector? Nonprofits will benefit by tailoring content and marketing for mobile devices and applications. Mobile websites or mobile-optimized web pages will help to meet growing demand.

Acknowledgments

I want to thank my parents, who are both gone now, for their unconditional love, guidance, and support. Dad, you always encouraged me to write a book and here it is! I especially want to thank my loving wife, Amy, and daughter, Natalie, for their understanding and inspiration during the many months of research and writing of this publication. In addition, I extend special appreciation to my sister (Janet) and brother (Steve) and friends for always being there and believing in me.

Of course, it takes many people to bring a book to print. I am grateful to Steve Simon, who helped edit the book, to Amy Quach, who designed the cover and other graphic elements, and Ryan Shapiro Photography.

I would also like to express particular appreciation to several nonprofits and individuals who enriched this book with their knowledge, review, and contributions. The nonprofits include the American Red Cross (Wendy Harman); FoodLink for Tulare County (Sandy Beals); Lutheran Services in America (Jill Schumann and Jeanean Merkel); Montgomery County Collaboration Council for Children, Youth and Families, Inc. (Carol Walsh); Network for Good (Bill Strathmann); NTEN (Holly Ross); TechSoup (Glenn Hirsch); and YMCA (Sara Ryan). I also would like to acknowledge Larry Checco, author of Branding for Success, for his review and comments.

INSPIRE GOOD is dedicated to nonprofit organizations everywhere that support worthy causes. The extraordinary work and tireless efforts of nonprofit staff and volunteers help to improve quality of life, strengthen communities, and make the world a better place for us all.

Notes

Chapter 1

American Red Cross, Interview with Wendy Harman, August 2010.
BlogPulse, *The Nielsen Company*, Number of public blogs (Fact),
November 2011.
Centers for Disease Control and Prevention, website, social media
sources, July 2011.
Corporation for National and Community Service. (Facts).
English Wikipedia: Number of articles (Fact), November 2011.
Facebook, Number of active users (Fact), November 2011.
Gladwell, Malcolm, *The Tipping Point: How Little Things Can Make a
Big Difference*, Little, Brown and Company, Back Bay Books, 2000.
Historical Statistics of the United States. Millennial Edition,
Cambridge University Press. (Fact).
NTEN Nonprofit Social Network Benchmark Report, March 2011.
Pew Research Center for the People and the Press, national survey,
media, March 2011.
U.S. Department of Health and Human Services, website, social
media sources, July 2011.
YouTube, video hours uploaded (Fact), November 2011.
Wikipedia, Number of articles posted (Fact), November 2011.
Wikipedia, definition of butterfly effect and chaos theory, July 2011.

Notes

Chapter 2

Ad Council, Smokey Bear campaign, April 2011.
American Express, website, cause marketing, history, April 2011.
American Heart Association, *Go Red for Women Campaign*, website, March 2011.
American Marketing Association, definition, March 2011.
Cone, Duke University *Behavioral Cause Study*, October 2008.
Grunig, James, E. and Hunt, Todd, *Managing Public Relations*, Holt, Rinehart and Winston, 1984.
Hiebert, Ray, E., *Courtier of the Crowd: The Story of Ivy Lee*, Iowa State University Press, 1966
Kantar Media, brand tracking (fact), March 2011.
Kotler, Philip and Lee, Nancy R., *Social Marketing: Influencing Behaviors for Good*, Sage Publications, 2008.
National Highway Traffic Safety Administration (NHTSA), Click or Ticket, and Vince and Larry Dummies campaigns.
Public Relations Society of America, definition, March 2011.
USDA Forest Service, Woodsy Owl and Smokey Bear campaigns, March 2011.

Chapter 3

Federal Emergency Management Agency (FEMA), Boy Scouts of America, Minor League Baseball Campaign, news release, July, 2009.
Convio Online Marketing Benchmark Index Study, March 2011.
Giving USA 2011: The Annual Report on Philanthropy for the Year 2010. Giving USA Foundation
Network for Good Case Study, online giving, October 2010.
NTEN profiled from nten.org.

TechSoup.org profiled from techsoup.org.
Volunteers of America, Major League Baseball Player Trust campaign, news release, May 2011.
McLuhan, Marshall, *Understanding Media: The Extensions of Man*, McGraw Hill, 1964.
Phillips, Donald, *Lincoln on Leadership*, Warner Books, 1992.
Seuss, Dr., (Theodor Seuss Geisel), *The Sneetches and Other Stories*, Random House, 1961.

Chapter 4

Aristotle, *The Art of Rhetoric*, Penguin Books, 1991.
Cone Nonprofit Power Brand 100 study, 2009.
FoodLink for Tulare County profiled from foodlink.org., June 2011
Gobe, Marc, *A New Brand World*, Penguin Books, 2002.
Trout, Jack, *Differentiate or Die: Survival in Our Era of Killer Competition*, John Wiley and Sons, Inc., 2000.
YMCA branding, provided by YMCA, June 2011.

Chapter 5

Bedbury, Scott, *A New Brand World, 8 Principles for Achieving Brand Leadership in the 21st Century*, Penguin Books, 2002.
Godin, Seth, *Purple Cow: Transform Your Business by Being Remarkable*, Penguin Group, 2002.
Nike website, corporate history, June 2011.

Chapter 6

Edwards, Betty, *The New Drawing on the Right Side of the Brain*, Jeremy P. Tarcher/Penguin, 1999.
Neumeier, Marty, *The Brand Gap*, New Riders, 2006.
Nietzsche, Friedrich, *The Birth of Tragedy: Out of the Spirit of Music*, Penguin Books, 1993, originally published 1872.
Wikipedia, Harvey Ball, http://en.wikipedia.org/wiki/Harvey_Ball, July 2011.

Notes

Chapter 7

Fogarty, Mignon, *Quick and Dirty Tips for Better Writing: Quick and Dirty Tips for Better Writing*, Henry Holt and Company, LLC, 2008.
Gordon, Karen Elizabeth, *The Deluxe Transitive Vampire: The Ultimate Handbook of Grammar for the Innocent, the Eager, and the Doomed*, Pantheon Books, 1993.
Strunk, Willliam, Jr. and White, E.B., *The Elements of Style*, Fourth Edition, WLC Books, 2009.

Chapter 8

Ries, Al and Trout, Jack, *Positioning: The Battle for Your Mind*, McGraw-Hill, 2001.
Edelman Trust Barometer, 2011.
University of Michigan, Study, Smoking Cessation, 2011.

Chapter 9

U.S. Census, Source, 2010 data.

Chapter 10

Useit.com, Jakob Nielsen's Website, June 2011.

Chapter 11

State of the News Media, Pew Research Center's Project for Excellence in Journalism, 2011.
Technorati, State of the Blogosphere, 2010.

Chapter 12

American Red Cross website, history, July 2011.
Nielsen Global Online Consumer Survey, 2009.
Outdoor Advertising Association of America website, July 2011.
U.S. Census, Source, 2010 data.
Word of Mouth Marketing Association, website, July 2011.

Chapter 13

Nonprofit Social Network Benchmark Report, NTEN, Common Knowledge, Blackbaud, 2011.
BlogPulse, *The Nielsen Company*, Number of public blogs (Fact), July 2011.
Facebook website, November 2011.
Flickr website, July 2011.
Mobile Internet Report, Morgan Stanley, December 2009.
Twitter website, November 2011.
YouTube website, November 2011.

Bibliography

Andresen, Katya, *Robin Hood Marketing: Stealing Corporate Savvy to Sell Just Causes*: Jossey-Bass, 2006.

Aristotle, *The Art of Rhetoric*, Penguin Books, 1991.

Bedbury, Scott, *A New Brand World, 8 Principles for Achieving Brand Leadership in the 21st Century*, Penguin Books, 2002.

Checco, Larry, *Branding for Success*, Trafford Publishing, 2005.

Daw Jocelyne and Carol Cone: *Breakthrough Nonprofit Branding*: John Wiley & Sons, Inc., 2010.

Durham, Sarah, *Brandraising*: Jossey-Bass, 2010.

Edwards, Betty, *The New Drawing on the Right Side of the Brain*, Jeremy P. Tarcher/Penguin, 1999.

Fogarty, Mignon, *Grammar Girl: Quick and Dirty Tips for Better Writing*, Henry Holt and Company, LLC, 2008.

Gladwell, Malcolm, *The Tipping Point: How Little Things Can Make a Big Difference*, Little, Brown and Company, Back Bay Books, 2000.

Gobe, Marc, *A New Brand World*, Penguin Books, 2002.

Godin, Seth, *Purple Cow: Transform Your Business by Being Remarkable*, Penguin Group, 2002.

Gordon, Karen Elizabeth, *The Deluxe Transitive Vampire: The Ultimate Handbook of Grammar for the Innocent, the Eager, and the Doomed*, Pantheon Books, 1993.

Grunig, James, E. and Hunt, Todd, *Managing Public Relations*, Holt, Rinehart and Winston, 1984.

Hamilton, Edith, *Mythology: Timeless Takes of Gods and Heroes*, Grand Central Publishing, 1999.

Heath, Chip and Heath, Dan, *Made to Stick: Why Some Ideas Survive and Others Die*, 2007.

Hiebert, Ray, E., *Courtier of the Crowd: The Story of Ivy Lee*, Iowa State University Press, 1966

Kotler, Philip and Lee, Nancy R., *Social Marketing: Influencing Behaviors for Good*, Sage Publications, 2008.

Laermer, Richard, *Full Frontal PR: Getting People Talking About You, Your Business or Your Product*, Bloomberg Press, 2003.

Leroux Miller, Kivi. *The Nonprofit Marketing Guide*: Jossey-Bass, 2010.

McLuhan, Marshall, *Understanding Media: The Extensions of Man*, McGraw Hill, 1964.

Neumeier, Marty, *The Brand Gap*, New Riders, 2006.

Nietzsche, Friedrich, *The Birth of Tragedy: Out of the Spirit of Music*, Penguin Books, 1993, originally published 1872.

Phillips, Donald, *Lincoln on Leadership*, Warner Books, 1992.

Ries, Al and Trout, Jack, *Positioning: The Battle for Your Mind*, McGraw-Hill, 2001.

Roberts, Kevin, *Lovemarks: The Future Beyond Brands*, 2004.

Seuss, Dr., (Theodor Seuss Geisel), *The Sneetches and Other Stories*, Random House, 1961.

Solis, Brian and Breakenridge, Deirdre, *Putting the Public Back in Public Relations*, FT Press, 2009.

Strunk, Willliam, Jr. and White, E.B., *The Elements of Style*, Fourth Edition, WLC Books, 2009.

Trout, Jack, *Differentiate or Die: Survival in Our Era of Killer Competition*, John Wiley and Sons, Inc., 2000.

Index

CPSIA information can be obtained at www.ICGtesting.com
Printed in the USA
LVOW080415190112

264584LV00001B/198/P